What I Wish I Knew When I Was 20

What I Wish I Knew When I Was 20

A Crash Course on Making Your Place in the World

Tina Seelig

HarperOne
An Imprint of HarperCollins*Publishers*

HarperOne

HarperCollins books may be purchased for educational, business, or sales promotional use. For information please write: Special Markets Department, HarperCollins Publishers, 10 East 53rd Street, New York, NY 10022.

HarperCollins Web site: http://www.harpercollins.com

FIRST EDITION

Designed by Level C

Library of Congress Cataloging-in-Publication Data
Seelig, Tina Lynn.
What I wish I knew when I was 20 : a crash course on making your place in the world / Tina L. Seelig. — 1st ed.
p. cm.
Includes bibliographical references.
ISBN 978-0-06-173519-6
1. Career education—United States. 2. School-to-work transition—United States. 3. Entrepreneurship. 4. Technological innovations. 5. Creative ability. I. Title. II. Title: What I wish I knew when I was 20.
LC1037.5.S44 2009
370.113—dc22 2009004879

11 12 13 RRD(H) 10 9 8 7

For Josh,
Happy 20th Birthday

CONTENTS

What I Wish I Knew When I Was 20

Chapter 1

BUY ONE, GET TWO FREE

What would you do to earn money if all you had was five dollars and two hours? This is the assignment I gave students in one of my classes at Stanford University. Each of fourteen teams received an envelope with five dollars of "seed funding" and was told they could spend as much time as they wanted planning. However, once they cracked open the envelope, they had two hours to generate as much money as possible. I gave them from Wednesday afternoon until Sunday evening to complete the assignment. Then, on Sunday evening, each team had to send me one slide describing what they had done, and on Monday afternoon each team had three minutes to present their project to the class. They were encouraged to be entrepreneurial by identifying opportunities, challenging assumptions, leveraging the limited resources they had, and by being creative.

What would you do if you were given this challenge? When I ask this question to most groups, someone usually shouts out, "Go to Las Vegas," or "Buy a lottery ticket." This gets a big laugh. These folks would take a significant risk in return for a small chance at earning a big reward. The next most common suggestion is to set up a car wash or lemonade stand, using the five dollars to purchase the starting materials. This is a fine option for those interested in earning a few extra dollars of spending money in two hours. But most of my students eventually found a way to move far beyond the standard responses. They took seriously the challenge to question traditional assumptions—exposing a wealth of possibilities—in order to create as much value as possible.

How did they do this? Here's a clue: the teams that made the most money didn't use the five dollars at all. They realized that focusing on the money actually framed the problem way too tightly. They understood that five dollars is essentially nothing and decided to reinterpret the problem more broadly: What can we do to make money if we start with absolutely nothing? They ramped up their observation skills, tapped into their talents, and unlocked their creativity to identify problems in their midst—problems they experienced or noticed others experiencing—problems they might have seen before but had never thought to solve. These problems were nagging but not necessarily at the forefront of anyone's mind. By unearthing these problems and then working to solve them, the winning teams brought in over $600, and the average return on the five dollar investment was 4,000 percent! If you take into account that many of the teams didn't use the funds at all, then their financial returns were infinite.

So what did they do? All of the teams were remarkably inventive. One group identified a problem common in a lot of college towns—the frustratingly long lines at popular restaurants on Saturday night. The team decided to help those people who didn't want to wait in line. They paired off and booked reservations at several restaurants. As the times for their reservations approached, they sold each reservation for up to twenty dollars to customers who were happy to avoid a long wait.

As the evening wore on, they made several interesting observations. First, they realized that the female students were better at selling the reservations than the male students, probably because customers were more comfortable being approached by the young women. They adjusted their plan so that the male students ran around town making reservations at different restaurants while the female students sold those places in line. They also learned that the entire operation worked best at restaurants that use vibrating pagers to alert customers when their table is ready. Physically swapping pagers made customers feel as though they were receiving something tangible for their money. They were more comfortable handing over their money and pager in exchange for the new pager. This had an additional bonus—teams could then sell the newly acquired pager as the later reservation time grew nearer.

Another team took an even simpler approach. They set up a stand in front of the student union where they offered to measure bicycle tire pressure for free. If the tires needed filling, they added air for one dollar. At first they thought they were taking advantage of their fellow students, who could easily go to a nearby gas station to have their tires filled. But after their first few customers, the students realized that the bicyclists were incredibly grateful. Even though the cyclists could get their tires filled for free nearby, and the task was easy for the students to perform, they soon realized that they were providing a convenient and valuable service. In fact, halfway through the two-hour period, the team stopped asking for a specific payment and requested donations instead. Their income soared. They made much more when their customers were reciprocating for a free service than when asked to pay a fixed price. For this team, as well as for the team making restaurant reservations, experimenting along the way paid off. The iterative process, where small changes are made in response to customer feedback, allowed them to optimize their strategy on the fly.

Each of these projects brought in a few hundred dollars, and their fellow classmates were duly impressed. However, the team that generated the greatest profit looked at the resources at their disposal through completely different lenses, and made $650. These students determined that the most valuable asset they had was neither the five dollars nor the two hours. Instead, their insight was that their most precious resource was their three-minute presentation time on Monday. They decided to sell it to a company that wanted to recruit the students in the class. The team created a three-minute "commercial" for that company and showed it to the students during the time they would have presented what they had done the prior week. This was brilliant. They recognized that they had a fabulously valuable asset—that others didn't even notice—just waiting to be mined.

Each of the other eleven teams found clever ways to earn money, including running a photo booth at the annual Viennese Ball, selling maps that highlighted local restaurants during Parents' Weekend, and designing and selling a custom T-shirt to the students in the class. One team actually lost money when the students purchased umbrellas to sell in San Francisco on a rainy day, only to have the weather clear up shortly after they launched their effort. And, yes, one team ran a car wash and another started a lemonade stand, but their returns were much lower than average.

I count the "Five-Dollar Challenge" as a success in teaching students about having an entrepreneurial mind-set. But it left me feeling a bit uncomfortable. I didn't want to communicate that value is always measured in terms of financial rewards. So, I added a twist the next time I assigned the project. Instead of five dollars, I gave each team an envelope containing ten paper clips. Teams were told they had four hours over the next few days to generate as much "value" as possible using the paper clips, where value could be measured in any way they wanted. The inspiration for this was the story of Kyle MacDonald, who started with one red paper clip and traded up until he had a house.[1] He set up a blog to document his progress and to solicit trades. It took a year, but step-by-step he reached his goal. He traded the red paper clip for a fish-shaped pen. He then traded the pen for a doorknob and the doorknob for a Coleman stove, and so on. The value of the items increased slowly but surely over the year until he had his dream house. Considering what Kyle did with one paper clip, I felt quite generous giving the students ten paper clips. The assignment began on a Thursday morning and presentations were scheduled for the following Tuesday.

By the time Saturday rolled around, however, I was anxious. Perhaps I'd gone too far this time. I worried the assignment would be a bust and was ready to chalk it up to experience. These concerns couldn't have been further from the mark. The seven student teams each chose to measure "value" in different ways. One decided that paper clips were the new currency and went about collecting as many as possible. Another team learned that the current world record for the longest paper clip chain was over twenty-two miles and set out to break that record. They rallied their friends and roommates, pitched local stores and businesses on their plan, and showed up in class with a mountain of paper clips linked together. Apparently the students in their dorm were so moved by the challenge that they committed themselves to breaking the world record even after the assignment was over. (I'm pretty sure they didn't break the record, but it's a good measure of the energy the team was able to generate.)

The most entertaining and provocative team came to class with a short video, with the song "Bad Boys" blaring in the background, that showed them using the paper clips to pick locks and break into dorm rooms to steal tens of thousands of dollars worth of sunglasses, cell phones, and computers. Just before I fainted, they announced that they were joking and showed another video documenting what they really had done. They traded the paper clips for some poster board and set up a stand at a nearby shopping center with a sign that read, "Stanford Students For Sale: Buy One, Get Two Free." They were amazed by the offers they received. They started out carrying heavy bags for shoppers, moved on to taking out the recycling from a clothing store, and eventually did an ad hoc brainstorming session for a woman who needed help solving a business problem. She paid them with three computer monitors she didn't need.

Over the years, I've continued to give groups similar assignments, changing the starting material from paper clips to Post-it® notes, or rubber bands, or water bottles. Each time the students surprise me, and themselves, by what they accomplish with limited time and resources. For example, using one small package of Post-it notes, students created a collaborative music project, a campaign to educate people about heart disease, and a public service commercial—called *Unplug-It*—about saving energy. This exercise ultimately evolved into what has become known as the "Innovation Tournament," with hundreds of teams from all over the world participating.[2] In each case, participants use the competition as a means to look at the world around them with fresh eyes, identifying opportunities in their own backyard. They challenge traditional assumptions, and in doing so generate enormous value from practically nothing. The entire adventure with Post-it notes was captured on film and became the foundation for a professional documentary called *Imagine It*.[3]

The exercises described above highlight several counterintuitive points. First, opportunities are abundant. At any place and time you can look around and identify problems that need solving. Some are mundane, such as scoring a table at a popular restaurant or pumping up bike tires. Many, as we well know, are much larger, relating to major world issues. As Vinod Khosla, a co-founder of Sun Microsystems and a successful venture capitalist, says so clearly, "The bigger the problem, the bigger the opportunity. Nobody will pay you to solve a non-problem."[4]

Second, regardless of the size of the problem, there are usually creative ways to use the resources already at your disposal to solve them. This is actually the definition many of my colleagues use for entrepreneurship: an entrepreneur is someone who is always on the lookout for problems that can be turned into opportunities and finds creative ways to leverage limited resources to reach their goals. Most people approach problems as though they can't be solved and, therefore, don't see the creative solutions sitting right in front of them.

Third, we so often frame problems too tightly. When given a simple challenge, such as earning money in two hours, most people quickly jump to standard responses. They don't step back and look at the problem more broadly. Taking off the blinders opens up a world of possibilities. Students who participated in these projects took this lesson to heart. Many reflected afterward that they would never have an excuse for being broke, since there is always a nearby problem begging to be solved.

These assignments grew out of a course I teach on entrepreneurship and innovation at Stanford University. The overarching goal is to demonstrate that all problems can be viewed as opportunities for creative solutions. I focus first on individual creativity, then move on to creativity in teams, and finally dive into creativity and innovation in large organizations. I give my students small challenges and slowly make them more difficult. As the course progresses, the students grow increasingly comfortable seeing problems through the lens of possibility and are eventually willing to take on just about anything that comes their way.

I've been at Stanford for ten years as the executive director of the Stanford Technology Ventures Program (STVP),[5] which is located in the School of Engineering. Our mission is to teach scientists and engineers about entrepreneurship and to provide them with the tools they need to be entrepreneurial in whatever role they play. We believe, along with a growing number of universities around the world, that it isn't good enough for students to come out of school with a purely technical education. To be successful, they need to understand how to be entrepreneurial leaders in all working environments and in all parts of their lives.

STVP focuses on teaching, scholarly research, and outreach to students, faculty, and entrepreneurs around the world. We strive to create "T-shaped people," those with a depth of knowledge in at least one discipline and a breadth of knowledge about innovation and entrepreneurship that allows them to work effectively with professionals in other disciplines to bring their ideas to life.[6] No matter what their role, having an entrepreneurial mind-set is key to solving problems, from small challenges that face each of us every day to looming world crises that require the attention and efforts of the entire planet. In fact, entrepreneurship cultivates a range of important life skills, from leadership and team building to negotiation, innovation, and decision making.

I'm also on the faculty of the Hasso Plattner Institute of Design at Stanford, affectionately called the "d.school."[7] This cross-disciplinary program draws upon educators from across the entire university, including the Schools of Engineering, Medicine, Business, and Education. The institute was envisioned and launched by Stanford mechanical engineering professor David Kelley, who is also the founder of the design firm IDEO, known for creating wildly inventive products and experiences. All d.school courses are taught by at least two professors from different disciplines, and cover an endless array of topics, from design for extreme affordability to creating infectious action to design for agile aging. As part of the d.school teaching team, I've experienced the thrill of radical collaboration, extreme brainstorming, and rapid prototyping as we give our students and ourselves big, messy problems with more than one right answer.

This book draws upon the stories that come out of the classrooms at Stanford as well as from my prior experiences as a scientist, entrepreneur, management consultant, educator, and author. Other stories come from those who have taken a wide range of paths, including entrepreneurs, inventors, artists, and academics. I'm fortunate to be surrounded by those who have done remarkable things by challenging assumptions and are eager to share their tales of success and failure.

Many of the ideas presented here are the polar opposite of the lessons we are taught in a traditional education system. In fact, the rules that apply in school are often completely different from those in the outside world. This disparity causes incredible stress when we leave school and attempt to find our way. Gracefully bridging that gap to tackle real-world challenges can be extremely difficult, but it's doable with the right tools and mind-set.

In school, students are usually evaluated as individuals and graded on a curve. In short, when they win someone else loses. Not only is this stressful, but it isn't how most organizations work. Outside of school, people usually work on a team with a shared goal, and when they win so does everyone else. In fact, in the business world there are usually small teams embedded inside larger teams, and at every level the goal is to make everyone successful.

The typical classroom has a teacher who views his or her job as pouring information into the students' brains. The door to the room is closed and the chairs are bolted to the floor, facing the teacher. Students take careful notes, knowing they will be tested on the material later. For homework they are asked to read assigned material from a textbook and quietly absorb it on their own. This couldn't be any more different from life after college, where you are your own teacher, charged with figuring out what you need to know, where to find the information, and how to absorb it. In fact, real life is the ultimate open book exam. The doors are thrown wide open, allowing you to draw on endless resources around you as you tackle open-ended problems related to work, family, friends, and the world at large. Carlos Vignolo, a masterful professor at the University of Chile, told me that he provocatively suggests that students take classes from the worst teachers in their school because this will prepare them for life, where they won't have talented educators leading the way.

Additionally, in large classes, students are typically given multiple-choice tests with one right answer for every question, and the bubbles must be carefully filled in with number two pencils to make for easy grading. In sharp contrast, in most situations outside of school there are a multitude of answers to every question, many of which are correct in some way. And, even more important, it is acceptable to fail. In fact, failure is an important part of life's learning process. Just as evolution is a series of trial-and-error experiments, life is full of false starts and inevitable stumbling. The key to success is the ability to extract the lessons out of each of these experiences and to move on with that new knowledge.

For most people, the world is quite different than a typical classroom. There isn't one right answer that leads to a clear reward, and facing the wall of choices in front of each of us can be quite overwhelming. Although family, friends, and neighbors will happily give us pointed advice about what to do, it is essentially our responsibility to pick our own direction. But it is helpful to know that we don't have to be right the first time. Life presents everyone with many opportunities to experiment and recombine our skills and passions in new and surprising ways.

The concepts presented in this book turn many well-worn ideas on their heads. My hope is to challenge you to see yourself and the world in a fresh light. The ideas are straightforward, but not necessarily intuitive. As an educator focusing on innovation and entrepreneurship, I have seen firsthand that these ideas are relevant to those working in dynamic environments, where situations change rapidly, requiring those involved to know how to identify opportunities, balance priorities, and learn from failure. Additionally, the concepts are valuable to anyone who wants to squeeze the most juice out of life.

In the coming chapters I will tell stories that come from a wide variety of sources, from recent college graduates to seasoned professionals. Hopefully, some of their experiences will resonate with you, providing insights and inspiration as you consider the choices you face throughout your life. Essentially, the goal of this book is to provide a new lens through which to view the obstacles you encounter every day while charting your course into the future. It is designed to give you permission to question conventional wisdom and to revisit the rules around you. There will always be uncertainty at each turn, but armed with the confidence that comes from seeing how others have coped with similar ambiguities, the stress will morph into excitement, and the challenges you face will become opportunities.

Chapter 2

THE UPSIDE-DOWN CIRCUS

Why don't most of us view problems as opportunities in our everyday lives? Why did the teams described previously have to wait for a class assignment to stretch the limits of their imaginations? Essentially, we aren't taught to embrace problems. We're taught that problems are to be avoided, or something to complain about. In fact, while speaking at a conference for business executives, I presented video clips from the Innovation Tournament as part of my talk. Later that afternoon the CEO of a company approached me and lamented that he wished he could go back to school, where he would be given open-ended problems and be challenged to be creative. I looked at him with confusion. I'm pretty confident that every day he faces real-life challenges that would benefit from creative thinking. Unfortunately, he didn't see that the concepts easily relate to his life and business. He viewed my assignments as something that could only happen in a controlled, academic environment. Of course, that isn't and shouldn't be the case at all.

We can challenge ourselves every single day. That is, we can choose to view the world through different lenses—lenses that allow us to see problems in a new light. The more we take on problems, the more confident and proficient we become at solving them. And the better able we are to see them as opportunities.

Attitude is perhaps the biggest determinant of what we can accomplish. True innovators face problems directly and turn traditional assumptions on their head. A wonderful example is Jeff Hawkins, who revolutionized the way people organize their lives with the Palm Pilot. Jeff was drawn to the problem of creating small personal computers that were easily accessible to the general public. This was a grand goal, and along the way he faced an endless array of additional challenges. In fact, he admits that being an entrepreneur means constantly facing big problems and finding creative ways to tame them.

Jeff's problems began at the very beginning. When Palm released its first product, the Zoomer, it failed miserably. Instead of walking away in defeat, Jeff and his team called the customers who had purchased the Zoomer, as well as those who had purchased its rival, the Apple Newton, and asked what they had hoped it would do. The customers said they had expected the product to organize their complicated schedules, helping them integrate several calendars into one. That's when Jeff realized the Zoomer was competing much more with paper calendars than with other computer products. This surprising feedback, which contradicted his original assumptions, provided useful input for the design of the next-generation product, the fabulously successful Palm Pilot.

Along the way, Jeff and his team tackled the daunting problem of determining how users would enter information into the new, small device. Jeff felt it was critically important to allow people to use a pen to enter information, in addition to a tiny keyboard, to make this process more natural. But handwriting-recognition programs of the day weren't up to the task. So Jeff and his team created a new written language, Graffiti, which was easier for the computer to recognize. There was considerable resistance inside the company to mandating the use of a new language, but Jeff was confident customers would spend a small amount of time up front in return for saving lots of time going forward. Graffiti was a radical innovation that challenged all the rules and solved a real problem.

Jeff Hawkins is a perfect example of a problem solver who is willing to look at the world with a fresh eye. His most recent company, Numenta, is built around his own theories about how the brain works. Jeff spent years teaching himself neuroscience in an attempt to understand how we think, and came up with a compelling and provocative theory about how the neocortex processes information, which he describes in his book *On Intelligence*. With these theories in hand, Jeff decided to use his ideas as the foundation for a "smarter" computer that processes information like the human brain. Of course, one could argue that Jeff Hawkins is one-of-a-kind, and that we can't all develop revolutionary theories and groundbreaking inventions. But it is much more productive to see Jeff as a source of inspiration, as someone who demonstrates that problems can be solved if we give ourselves permission to look at them differently.

Why don't we all focus on the opportunities that surround us each day and take full advantage of them? One project that came out of the second Innovation Tournament sheds some light on this idea. During the tournament, participants were challenged to create as much value as possible with rubber bands. One team came up with the idea for "Do Bands," bracelets that give people a simple incentive to "do" the things they often put off doing. Do Bands is a clever idea, inspired by the now-familiar rubber bracelets worn to show solidarity with a cause, such as Lance Armstrong's Live Strong bracelets. Do Bands have a few guiding principles:

- Put one around your wrist with a promise to do something.
- Take it off when you have completed the task.

- Record your success online at the Do Bands Web site. Each Do Band comes with a number printed on it so you can look up all the actions it has inspired.

- Pass the Do Band along to someone else.

Do Bands give individuals an incentive to do what they wanted to do all along. In reality, a Do Band is just a rubber band. But sometimes something as simple as a rubber band is all that's needed to mobilize people to actually do something, to bridge the gap between inaction and action. The Do Bands campaign only lasted a few days, but in that short time it inspired a long list of actions: Some people called their mothers, some showed their appreciation to others by sending thank-you notes, and one began a new exercise program. One participant used the Do Band as an impetus to start a summer camp, one was inspired to reach out to long-lost friends, and some donated money to charities of their choice. It's fascinating that a rubber band was all that was needed to move people to act. It's also a clear reminder that there is just a tiny switch between doing nothing and doing something, but that the two options have wildly different outcomes.

I assign a simple challenge in my class, using a related concept, that's designed to give students experience looking at obstacles in their lives from a new perspective. I ask them to identify a problem, and then pick a random object in their environment. They then need to figure out how that object will help them solve the problem. Of course, I have no notion about their personal challenges, what objects they will select, or whether they will successfully solve their problem. However, in most cases they manage to find a way to use random objects in their environment to tackle a seemingly unrelated problem.

My favorite example is a young woman who was moving from one apartment to another. She had to transport some large furniture and had no idea how to make it happen. If she couldn't move the furniture, she would have to leave it in her old apartment. She looked around her apartment and saw a case of wine that was left over from a party a few weeks earlier. Aha! She went to craigslist®, an online community bulletin board, and offered to trade the case of wine for a ride across the Bay Bridge with her furniture. Within a few hours, all of her furniture was moved. The leftover wine collecting dust in the corner had been transformed into valuable currency. The assignment didn't turn the wine into currency, but it did give this woman the ability and motivation to see it that way.

There is no limit to the size of the problems you can tackle. In fact, most of the Innovation Tournament projects were crafted to create "social value." That is, students used the competition as an opportunity to address a significant social problem, such as saving energy, encouraging people to stay healthy, or providing community support for disabled children.

The first step to solving big problems is to identify them. In the world of product design, this is called "need finding." This is a skill that can be learned. In fact, it's a key component of the curriculum for the BioDesign Fellows at Stanford.[1] Postgraduates who have studied engineering, medicine, and business come together for a year to identify significant needs in medicine and then design products to address them. Paul Yock, a cardiologist, inventor, and entrepreneur, runs the BioDesign Program.[2] Paul believes that "a well-characterized need is the DNA of an invention." In other words, if we clearly define a problem, the solution will logically present itself.

The BioDesign Fellows spend three months shadowing doctors in action and identifying problems they appear to be facing. They watch carefully; talk with all of the stakeholders, including physicians, nurses, patients, and administrators; and figure out where things can be improved. They whittle a list of hundreds of needs to just a handful, with the goal of picking the biggest problems they can find. After they settle on the challenge, they design and quickly build prototypes for a variety of solutions. After a focused, iterative process, they present their new product concepts to the key stakeholders to find out if they have successfully met the need.

Interestingly, in many cases those who are on the front lines are so used to the problems they experience every day that they don't even see them, or can't imagine radical approaches to solving them. Paul Yock shared a story about the development of balloon angioplasty, a technique that involves inserting a balloon into an artery and expanding it so that it opens up the blocked artery. Before this breakthrough invention, most cardiologists felt that the only way to deal with clogged arteries was to do bypass surgery to remove the damaged blood vessels. This procedure requires open-heart surgery, which carries substantial risks. When the balloon angioplasty procedure, which is much less dangerous and invasive, was first introduced, it was met with tremendous skepticism and resistance among physicians, especially surgeons who "understood best" how to treat the disease. Significant roadblocks appeared in front of pioneers of the procedure. For example, John Simpson, one of the inventors of balloon angioplasty, wound up having to leave the university to do his research at a private hospital. However, over time, the efficacy of balloon angioplasty was firmly established and became the standard of care for most patients with clogged arteries. This is a great example of a case where the status quo is so entrenched that those closest to the situation can't imagine anything different.

"Problem blindness" applies to consumer product development as well. For example, it is well documented that automatic teller machines (ATMs) failed in focus groups where potential customers were asked if they would use a machine to deposit and withdraw money from their accounts, as opposed to going into a local bank to complete the transaction with a teller. These customers couldn't imagine changing their behavior so dramatically. But, in retrospect, ATM machines represented a radically new and effective improvement for personal banking, one that few of us can now imagine living without.

I've experienced problem blindness myself. About fifteen years ago my husband, Mike, gave me a cell phone. This was long before cell phones were ubiquitous, and I had no idea I needed one. In fact, I got somewhat annoyed, thinking it was one more electronic gadget that would sit around unused. Mike urged me to try it for a week. It took me only two days to figure out I couldn't live without it. I was commuting at least two hours each day and was able to catch up with friends and colleagues during the drive. I came back to Mike with sincere appreciation for the gift, and now always try to keep this story in mind when I look at new, potentially breakthrough, ideas.

The key to need finding is identifying and filling gaps—that is, gaps in the way people use products, gaps in the services available, and gaps in the stories they tell when interviewed about their behavior. I got a chance to talk with Michael Barry, an expert in need finding at Point Forward, and he told a terrific story about his work with Kimberly-Clark, the company that makes Kleenex®, Scott® paper towels, and Huggies® diapers. Essentially, Kimberly-Clark was disappointed with their diaper sales relative to diaper giants such as Procter & Gamble (makers of Pampers), and brought in Michael's team to help figure out how they could improve their business. By making detailed observations on how diapers are sold, assessing the messaging on the diaper packages, and conducting interviews with parents, Michael realized that Kimberly-Clark was missing the point: they were selling diapers as though they were hazardous waste disposal devices. But parents don't view them that way. To a parent, a diaper is a way to keep their children comfortable. Dealing with diapers is part of the nurturing process. A diaper is also viewed as a piece of clothing. These observations provided a great starting point for improving how Kimberly-Clark packaged and positioned Huggies. Then, upon closer scrutiny, Michael identified an even *bigger* opportunity. He noticed that parents become terribly embarrassed when asked if their child is "still in diapers." Bingo! This was a huge pain point for parents and for kids on the cusp of toilet training. There had to be a way to turn this around. How could a diaper become a symbol of success as opposed to failure? Michael came up with the idea for Pull-Ups®, a cross between a diaper and underwear. Switching from diapers to Pull-Ups served as a big milestone for both children and parents. A child can put on a Pull-Up without help, and can feel proud of this accomplishment. This insight led to a billion-dollar increase in annual revenue for Kimberly-Clark and allowed them to leapfrog ahead of their competition. This new product grew out of focused need finding, identification of a clear problem, and then turning it an opportunity.

In my course, I use a case study about Cirque du Soleil[3] that gives students a chance to hone their skills at challenging assumptions. The backdrop is the 1980s, when the circus industry was in trouble. Performances were predictable and stale, the number of customers was diminishing, and animal treatment was under attack. It didn't seem like a good time to start a new circus, but that is exactly what Guy Laliberté, a street performer in Canada, decided to do. Guy started Cirque du Soleil by challenging every assumption about what a circus could be and in doing so transformed a problem—a dying industry—into an opportunity.

After showing video clips from the 1939 Marx Brothers movie, *At the Circus*, I ask the students to uncover all the assumptions of a traditional circus: a big tent, animals, cheap tickets, barkers selling souvenirs, several acts performing at once, playful music, clowns, popcorn, strong men, flaming hoops, etc. I then ask them to turn these things upside down—to imagine the exact opposite of each one. For example, the new list would include a small tent, no animals, expensive seats, no barkers, one act performing at a time, sophisticated music, and no clowns or popcorn. They then pick the things they want to keep from the traditional circus and the things they want to change. The result is a brand-new type of circus, à la Cirque du Soleil. I then show them video clips from recent Cirque du Soleil performances so they can see the impact of these changes. Once we do this exercise with the circus industry, it's easy to apply to other industries and institutions, including fast-food restaurants, hotels, airlines, sporting events, education, and even courtship and marriage.

Once you get the hang of it, this is an easy, back-of-the-envelope exercise you can use to reevaluate all aspects of your life and career. The key is to take the time to clearly identify every assumption. This is usually the hardest part, since, as described in the case about balloon angioplasty, assumptions are sometimes so integrated into our view of the world that it's hard to see them. However, with a little practice, it becomes a useful way to look at your options in a fresh light.

Some people are particularly good at identifying and challenging assumptions. In their quest to find creative solutions to seemingly impossible problems, they question the limits of what is reasonable and possible. They start their lives over in exotic locations, they take on projects that have a grand scope, they make choices that seem radical, and they carve out a new path that leads them into uncharted territory. We often watch in awe, preventing ourselves from taking the same leaps.

Consider Sandra Cook, who has successfully stretched the boundaries and challenged all traditional assumptions as she crafted amazing adventures for herself. The beginning of Sandra's career snapped into place like clockwork. She earned a PhD in mathematical logic, went off to the London School of Economics to study and then teach, came back to the United States to work at the Stanford Research Institute (SRI), took a job as a consultant at Booz Allen Hamilton, and eventually headed up strategy for the communications businesses for Motorola. She could have continued on this path for the rest of her career, but decided to jump out of this perfectly good airplane because it was heading in the wrong direction.

Sandra's passion has always been adventurous travel to wild and remote places, and she managed to squeeze exotic trips to India, Tibet, Mongolia, and Nepal into two-week stints during her busy work schedule. But she eventually decided this wasn't enough, and so flipped her world on its head by quitting her prestigious job at Motorola in 2002 in order to travel in Afghanistan more extensively. The country was in shambles after the war began, and she wanted to help in any way she could. She got a visa, purchased an airline ticket, and went, hoping to find some way to make a difference. When she got off the plane in Kabul, there were no taxis and little infrastructure in place. With some effort, she found her way to a hotel frequented by reporters from around the world, and got to work contacting everyone she could to find out how she could get involved with the effort to rebuild the country. She offered to write grants, to prepare business plans, or even to sweep floors—whatever would be helpful.

Sandra eventually connected with Nancy Dupree, the director of the Afghanistan Center at Kabul University. Nancy was working tirelessly to rebuild the university library and to get books into the hands of people throughout the country through their Box Library Extension. After they got to know each other a little better, Sandra wrote a business plan for the center and was eventually asked to serve on the organization's board of directors. She is now co-president of the board and spends most of her time building awareness of and raising money for this organization. Besides her official duties, Sandra also takes on grassroots projects in Afghanistan, such as distributing pomegranate trees throughout the city of Kabul. She personally purchased twenty thousand bare-root trees and handed them out to families so they could start replacing trees destroyed during the war.

Most people do not leave comfortable lives to tackle enormous problems in far-flung lands. But, in many cases, much smaller challenges seem just as daunting. For many, changing jobs or moving across town feels just as risky as traveling to an exotic location to perform relief work. It is much more comfortable to stay locked in a role that's "good enough" than to reach for an alternative that has a higher degree of uncertainty. Most of us are content taking small, reliable steps. We don't get very far, but we don't rock the boat either.

Venture capital firms that invest in early stage businesses pride themselves on identifying big problems and taking significant risks with the goal of tackling them. They are always scanning the horizon for the next big opportunity, as opposed to looking for small problems with incremental solutions. They attempt to look into the future for challenges that are just beyond the next hill so they can invest in radically innovative approaches to meeting them head-on. A great example is Kleiner Perkins Caufield & Byers (KPCB), a firm with a remarkable track record for predicting future challenges and investing in their solutions. They invested in biotechnology, Internet commerce, and alternative energy long before these were household topics, and they anticipated the future impact of businesses such as Genentech, Sun Microsystems, Amazon, Google, Netscape, Intuit, and Electronic Arts. As Randy Komisar, a partner at

KPCB, notes, being entrepreneurial means seeing the world as opportunity rich. He and his colleagues have found that identifying and solving big problems leads to significant rewards for everyone involved.

Despite the fact that one can make a profit by solving big problems, Randy stresses in his book, *The Monk and the Riddle,* the importance of having the zeal to solve a grand problem, as opposed to being motivated to make money.[4] To explain the difference, he compares a missionary who passionately pursues an important cause to a mercenary whose drive is only to serve his or her own interests. By focusing on finding solutions to significant challenges with missionary-like energy, successful companies are born. This message is echoed by author Guy Kawasaki, who says it is better to "make meaning than to make money."[5] If your goal is to make meaning by trying to solve a big problem in innovative ways, you are more likely to make money than if you start with the goal of making money, in which case you will probably not make money *or* meaning.

What do the entrepreneurs, venture capitalists, and inventors described above have to do with the students who started with five dollars, paper clips, or water bottles and were challenged to create as much value as possible? A tremendous amount. All of these examples reinforce the idea that there is great benefit to identifying problems in your midst and then relentlessly working to solve them by challenging traditional assumptions.

Problems are abundant, just waiting for those willing to find inventive solutions. This takes acute observation, coordinated teamwork, the ability to execute a plan, a willingness to learn from failure, and creative problem solving. But the first requirement is having the attitude that the problem can be solved. I have found, for myself and my students, that the more experience you have tackling problems, the more confident you become that you can find a solution.

I was recently in Scotland teaching in a weeklong entrepreneurship boot camp, run by James Barlow at the Scottish Institute for Enterprise, for fifty college students from across the country who were studying a wide range of disciplines, from criminology to cosmetics. Most of them had no exposure to entrepreneurship at all. At the beginning of the week, many were completely overwhelmed by the first assignment, which required them to come up with and then sell a new product or service. Each team was given fifty British pounds of starting capital at 6:00 p.m. and had a total of eighteen hours to complete the project. The goal was to get them out of their comfort zone and into the real world. Many of the students told me they were on the verge of going home. (They didn't need to tell me this, because the panicked looks on their faces said it all.) But they all stuck with it and were pleasantly shocked by what they accomplished. One group became "umbrella walkers," assisting those who got caught in the unexpected rain; one group set up an impromptu speed-dating station at a local bar; and one started a makeshift shoeshine stand on a busy downtown street.

But this assignment was just the beginning of their experience. By the end of a week's worth of challenging activities, including scouring newspapers to identify problems, brainstorming to come up with creative solutions, designing new ventures, meeting with potential customers, filming commercials, and pitching their ideas to a panel of successful executives, they were ready to take on just about any challenge.

One team that stands out in my mind was composed of three young women, for whom all of this was brand-new. They were shaking in their shoes when the first assignment was given. By the end of the week, however, they had come up with a fabulous idea that earned high praise from the panel of judges as well as seed funding from investors. They developed a mobile, at-home service for bra fitting, based on their observation that most women are embarrassed by the process and often end up with ill-fitting bras. Their video commercial was tasteful and convinced everyone that this was an interesting opportunity.

On the last day of the workshop, one of the young women said to me, "I now know that there isn't anything I can't do." She, along with all the other students, already had the bulk of the skills they needed to accomplish amazing things. All we offered them was tangible proof, along with a healthy dose of permission, that they could turn the problems around them into opportunities.

Chapter 3

BIKINI OR DIE

The famous psychologist B. F. Skinner once wrote that all human behavior can be viewed as being adaptive to either the individual, the gene pool, or to society at large.[1] However, these three forces are often at odds, causing significant tension. The rules made by society are a huge presence in our lives, created by the government, religious groups, our employers, our schools, our neighbors, and our families. Because these social groups craft the explicit rules around us, we often find ourselves in situations where we are driven to break them to satisfy our personal desires or the drives of our species. These social rules and norms are designed to make the world around us more organized and predictable, and to prevent us from hurting one another.

But when is a rule really just a suggestion? And when do suggestions morph into rules? Every day, physical signs tell all of us what to do, written instructions direct us how to behave, and social guidelines urge us to act within specific parameters.

In fact, we also make lots of rules for ourselves, in large part encouraged by others. These rules become woven into our individual fabric as we go through life. We draw imaginary lines around what we think we can do—lines that often limit us much more than the rules imposed by society at large. We define ourselves by our professions, our income, where we live, the car we drive, our education, and even by our horoscope. Each definition locks us into specific assumptions about who we are and what we can do. I'm reminded of a famous line from the movie *My Dinner with Andre,* that states that New Yorkers "are both guards and prisoners and as a result they no longer have . . . the capacity to leave the prison they have made, or even see it as a prison." We always make our own prisons, with rules that we each create for ourselves, locking us into specific roles and out of an endless array of possibilities. What if you challenge the underlying assumptions? What are the consequences—good and bad—of getting off the prescribed path? What happens to those who break the rules?

Larry Page, co-founder of Google, gave a lecture in which he encouraged the audience to break free from established guidelines by having a healthy disregard for the impossible.[2] That is, to think as big as possible. He noted that it is often easier to have big goals than to have small goals. With small goals, there are very specific ways to reach them and more ways they can go wrong. With big goals, you are usually allocated more resources and there are more ways to achieve them. This is an interesting insight. Imagine that you are trying to get from San Francisco to Kabul. There are lots of different routes, you will likely give yourself the time and resources to get there, and you will be flexible if things don't unfold as planned. But if your goal is to go across town, then the path is pretty clear and you expect it to be a quick trip. If the road is blocked for some reason, you are stuck and frustrated. One of the reasons Google has been so successful is their willingness to tackle hard problems with an undefined path to completion.

Linda Rottenberg is a prime example of a person who sees no problem as too big to tackle and readily breaks free of expectations in order to get where she wants to go. She believes that if others think your ideas are crazy, then you must be on the right track. Eleven years ago Linda started a remarkable organization called Endeavor.[3] Their goal is to foster entrepreneurship in the developing world. She launched Endeavor just after graduating from Yale Law School, with little more than a passion to stimulate economic development in disadvantaged regions. She stopped at nothing to reach her goals, including "stalking" influential business leaders whose support she needed.

Endeavor began its efforts in Latin America and has since expanded to other regions of the world, including Turkey and South Africa. They go through a rigorous process to identify high-potential entrepreneurs and, after selecting those with great ideas and the drive to execute their plan, give them the resources they need to be successful. The entrepreneurs are not handed money, but instead are introduced to those in their environment who can guide them. They are also provided with intense educational programs, and get an opportunity to meet with other entrepreneurs in their region who have navigated the circuitous path before. Once successful, they serve as positive role models, create jobs in their local communities, and, eventually, give back to Endeavor, helping future generations of entrepreneurs.

An inspiring example of an Endeavor entrepreneur is Leila Velez in Brazil. Leila lived in the slums in the hills overlooking Rio de Janiero, known as *favelas.* Cleaning houses, she survived on a subsistence income. However, she had an idea: there are many women in Brazil who want desperately to have softer, less kinky hair. Leila, along with her sister-in-law Heloisa Assis, invented a product that transforms knotty hair into curly hair. It took years of trial-and-error experimentation, resulting in many extreme failures along the way, but once she found a solution, she opened a salon in Rio. Her business was brisk and Leila had the fantasy of creating a franchise. Along came Endeavor, which helped her realize her dream. This business, called Beleza Natural, now employs a thousand people and earns millions in annual revenue.

This is but one of hundreds of success stories from Endeavor. I was at Endeavor's biannual summit two years ago and was overwhelmed with the energy and enthusiasm in the room. Each entrepreneur was indebted to Endeavor for providing the tools they needed, as well as the inspiration to succeed. This would never have happened if Linda had listened to those who told her that her ideas were crazy.

• • •

One of the biggest obstacles to taking on "impossible tasks" is that others are often quick to tell you they can't be accomplished. It is arguably tough to address a grand problem. But once you decide to take it on, it is equally hard to break out of traditional approaches to solving it. This is another place where it is helpful to break a few rules. The next exercise forces people to do this in a surprising way. First, come up with a problem that is relevant for the particular group. For example, if it is a group of executives in the utility business, the topic might be getting companies to save energy; if it is a theater group, the problem might be how to attract a larger audience; and if it is a group of business students, the challenge might be to come up with a cool, new business idea. Break the group into small teams and ask each one to come up with the best idea and the worst idea for solving the stated problem.[4] The best idea is something that each team thinks will solve the problem brilliantly. The worst idea will be ineffective, unprofitable, or will make the problem worse. Once they are done, they write each of their ideas on a separate piece of paper, one labeled BEST and one labeled WORST. When I do this exercise, I ask participants to pass both to me, and I proceed to shred the BEST ideas. After the time they spent generating these great ideas, they are both surprised and not too happy.

I then redistribute the WORST ideas. Each team now has an idea that another team thought was terrible. They are instructed to turn this bad idea into a fabulous idea. They look at the horrible idea that was passed their way and quickly see that it really isn't so bad after all. In fact, they often think it is terrific. Within a few seconds someone always says, "Hey, this is a great idea!"

When doing this exercise with a utility company, one of the "worst ideas" for saving energy was to give each employee a quota for how much energy he or she used and to charge extra for exceeding the allotment. They thought this was a pretty silly idea. The team that received this idea turned it into an idea that is really worth considering, in which employees *do* have a quota for how much energy they use. If they use less they get money back, and if they use more they are charged for it. They could even sell energy credits to their co-workers, giving them an even larger incentive to save electricity.

I did this exercise with the staff responsible for putting on arts events at Stanford. One of the teams charged with finding ways to bring in a larger audience came up with the "bad" idea of putting on a staff talent show. This is seemingly the opposite of what they do now—bringing in top-notch talent from around the world. The next team turned this idea upside down. They interpreted this much more broadly and proposed a big fund-raiser, where the faculty and staff across the university would showcase their diverse talents. This would very likely bring in lots of people who don't normally go to performing arts events and would help build awareness for their other programs.

When the challenge was to come up with the worst business idea, the suggestions were boundless. One group suggested selling bikinis in Antarctica, one recommended starting a restaurant that sells cockroach sushi, and one group proposed starting a heart attack museum. In each of these cases, these bad ideas were transformed into pretty interesting ideas that deserved some real consideration. For example, the group that was tasked with selling bikinis in Antarctica came up with the slogan "Bikini or Die." Their idea was to take people who wanted to get into shape on a trip to Antarctica. By the end of the hard journey, they would be able to fit into their bikinis. The group that needed to sell cockroach sushi came up with a restaurant called La Cucaracha that made all sorts of exotic sushi using nontraditional but nutritious ingredients and targeted adventurous diners. The group given the challenge of starting a heart attack museum used this idea as the starting point for a museum devoted entirely to health and preventative medicine. All groups came up with compelling business names, slogans, and commercials for these ventures.

This exercise is a great way to open your mind to solutions to problems because it demonstrates that most ideas, even if they look silly or stupid on the surface, often have at least a seed of potential. It helps to challenge the assumption that ideas are either good or bad, and demonstrates that, with the right frame of mind, you can look at most ideas or situations and find something valuable. For example, even if you don't start the "Bikini or Die" excursion to Antarctica, this is an interesting starting point for ideas that might be more practical.

• • •

My old buddy John Stiggelbout used the idea of turning a good idea on its head when applying to graduate school. He did something that any normal person would think was a terribly bad idea, and it turned out to be inspired. He decided at the last minute that he wanted to go to business school. Having missed all the deadlines, he chose to make his application stand out among the others in an unconventional way. Instead of touting his impressive accomplishments, as most applicants do, he augmented his traditional application with a letter of reference written by a past professor claiming to be John's best friend and cell mate in prison. The letter described John in the most unusual terms that any admissions committee had ever seen, including his ability to open a mason jar with his belch. Instead of knocking John out of the running, those in the admissions office were incredibly curious to meet him and invited John to visit the school. John was nice enough to dig up the letter so you can see it, too.

> I met John Stiggelbout as a fellow Greyhound bus passenger. He must have passed out on the floor at the back. I found him next to a Styrofoam cup and a candy wrapper, covered with cigarette butts, holding an empty MD 20/20 bottle. I am his best friend. We were cell mates after we got caught robbing the 7/11.
>
> After a hearty meal at the Salvation Army, we once went to a revival meeting where we were both

trying to pick up the same girl. (He takes defeat and humiliation well; he is obviously a practiced loser.)

He has impressive qualities that any struggling Junior Achievement Company or small family laundry could put to good use. He covers his brown and yellow teeth when he yawns, and opens the window when he spits. He can whistle loud using his fingers, and can crack a mason jar with his burp. He showers once a month. He uses soap when he can.

He needs a place so he doesn't have to sleep in the bus station restroom. He needs to find a position with a large company where his heavy drinking and sexual preference for exotic birds will not get him fired the first day on the job.

Anyone with a sexual preference for exotic birds is both original and independent of thought. In fact, he is so independent of thought that he is utterly devoid of it.

This guy will do anything for a drink. He may even work.

Now that Stiggs is out of jail, I'm sure his parole officer would not mind if some graduate school looked after him for a bit. He is a great leader in the Hells Angels, and all the boys I talked to thought he would make a hell of a white collar criminal.

Of all the people I have found on the floor, passed out in the back of a bus, this guy is the best.

> My overall impression is that he is not as good as I make him out to be. Get me out of jail so that I can go to Chicago instead of him.
>
> Buford T. Morton, Inmate #335342
> Walla Walla Federal Penitentiary
> Walla Walla, Washington

Once John arrived for the interview, everyone in the office was peeking out of his or her doors, hoping to get a look at the fellow who submitted the wild application. He was polite and poised during his interview, and was admitted.

The concept that there are no bad ideas is a hallmark of good brainstorming. During a brainstorming session it is important to explicitly state that there are no bad ideas. You need to break with the assumption that ideas need to be feasible in order to be valuable. By encouraging people to come up with wild ideas you diffuse the tendency to edit your ideas before you share them. Sometimes the craziest ideas, which seem impractical when they are initially proposed, turn out to be the most interesting in the long run. They might not work in their first iteration, but with a bit of massaging, they might turn out to be brilliant solutions that are feasible to implement.

Running a successful brainstorming session actually takes a lot of skill and practice. The key is to set the ground rules at the beginning and to reinforce them. Tom Kelley, general manager of the design firm IDEO and David Kelley's brother, wrote a book called *The Art of Innovation,* in which he describes the rules of brainstorming at their firm. One of the most important rules is to expand upon the ideas of others. With this approach, at the end of a good brainstorming session, multiple people feel that they created or contributed to the best ideas to come out of the session. And, since everyone in the room had a chance to participate and witnessed the emergence and evolution of all the ideas, there is usually shared support for the ideas that go forward toward implementation.

If you have participated in brainstorming sessions, you know that they don't always work like that. It is hard to eliminate the natural tendency for each person to feel personal ownership for their ideas, and it can be tough to get participants to build on others' suggestions. Patricia Ryan Madson, who wrote *Improv Wisdom,* designed a great warm-up exercise that brings to life these two ideas: there are no bad ideas *and* build on others' ideas. You break a group into pairs. One person tries to plan a party and makes suggestions to the other person. The other person has to say no to every idea and must give a reason why it won't work. For example, the first person might say, "Let's plan a party for Saturday night," and the second person would say, "No, I have to wash my hair." This goes on for a few minutes, as the first person continues to get more and more frustrated trying to come up with any idea the second person will accept. Once this runs its course, the roles switch and the second person takes on the job of planning a party. The first person has to say yes to everything and must build on the idea. For example, "Let's have a party on Saturday night." The response might be, "Yes, and I'll bring a cake." This goes on for a while and the ideas can get wilder. In some cases the parties end up under water or on another planet, and involve all sorts of exotic food and entertainment. The energy in the room increases, spirits are high, and a huge number of ideas are generated.

This is the type of energy that should be present during a great brainstorming session. Of course, at some point you have to decide what is feasible, but that shouldn't happen during the "idea generation" phase. Brainstorming is about breaking out of conventional approaches to solving a problem. You should feel free to flip ideas upside down, to turn them inside out, and to cut loose from the chains of normalcy. At the end of a brainstorming session you should be surprised by the range of ideas that were generated. In almost all cases, at least a few will serve as seeds for really great opportunities that are ripe for further exploration.

It is important to remember that idea generation involves exploration of the landscape of possibilities. It doesn't cost any money to generate wild ideas, and there is no need to commit to any of them. The goal is to break the rules by imagining a world where the laws of nature are different and all constraints are removed. Once this phase is complete, it is appropriate to move on to the "exploitation" phase, where you select some of the ideas to explore further. At that time you can view the ideas with a more critical eye.

• • •

Rule breaking can happen throughout every organization and in all processes. A great example can be found at Cooliris, a young company that creates an immersive Web browsing experience. Essentially, Cooliris turns the standard flat Web pages we view online into a three-dimensional wall that makes browsing a faster and more intuitive experience. The images stretch out in front of you, making you feel as though you're navigating through a gallery.

Two Stanford students, Josh Schwarzapel and Austin Shoemaker, started Cooliris with a seasoned entrepreneur, Souyanja Bhumkar. They received a small amount of funding for their venture, but were having a very difficult time recruiting people to work at the company. This was a big problem. They were never going to reach their aggressive product development goals unless they brought in dozens of talented people. And to make that happen, they were going to have to do things differently.

Josh, who was in charge of recruiting, started with all the traditional approaches to recruiting, including posting positions on job boards and craigslist, advertising on social networking sites such as LinkedIn and Facebook, and even hiring professional recruiters. But nothing was working. So the team decided to look at the entire recruiting situation differently, and to break with these standard approaches. Instead of trying to convince young, talented people to join the company, they decided to focus on making Cooliris such an appealing place to work that students would be begging to join. They wanted it to be the coolest "party" in town. They hosted special events for students, made sure to have the most dramatic booth at the job fairs, complete with eye-popping demos of their product on big plasma screens; and handed out hip sunglasses to everyone who visited their booth.

They also hired two Stanford students, Jonah Greenberg and Matt Wahl, as interns. Their job was to spread the word about Cooliris across the Stanford campus, and to identify the best students they could, independent of their age or field of study. Jonah and Matt are popular and well connected, and tapped into their social circles to spread the word about Cooliris. They helped make it cool to work at Cooliris, and eventually Cooliris became *the* place to be.

Now that Cooliris was inundated with résumés, how did they decide which students to hire? Instead of going through a rigorous screening process, they decided to *not* decide, and hired almost everyone—as interns. This gave them the chance to see each individual in action, and for the students to get a taste of the company. Not only did Cooliris get an opportunity to take the interns for a test drive, but the interns got so excited about the products that they became evangelists both for the product and the company, bringing in their friends as interns and as customers. This helped with recruiting and built momentum for the business.

Now that they were on a roll, Cooliris continued to break rules. They abolished the hierarchy between interns and full-time employees, giving interns significant projects with full accountability for their results. Each intern was given a project with a big goal and was allowed to do whatever he or she felt would work to reach it. Of course, there was oversight, but the interns were clearly empowered to make key decisions. For example, the goal might be to increase the number of Web sites that are Cooliris enabled. The interns weren't told what to do, but each was encouraged to run with his or her project. In this way, they could easily see what each person could accomplish and reward those who did an outstanding job.

But they didn't stop there. They also figured out that the best way to identify those who were a good fit for the company is to see them in action. To do that, they brought in hundreds of students for user-testing of their product. This is, of course, standard practice to evaluate new project features. But Cooliris also used product testing as a recruiting tool. During the interaction with each tester, they could see how each person thought and how passionate he or she was about the product and, ultimately, whether he or she would be a good fit with the company. At the very least they got useful customer feedback and at best they found a new employee.

You might think it's easier to challenge conventions and break rules as an individual or a small start-up firm, but you can also break the rules that get in the way from within a large company. I learned about the launch of Zune at Microsoft from a former student, Tricia Lee. This product, designed to compete with the Apple iPod, was on a tight development schedule. About halfway through the project, it was clear they weren't going to meet their aggressive goals. The software wasn't close to halfway complete, and on the current course—with the usual checks and balances, feedback loops, and bureaucracy—it was going to take much longer than expected to complete. To address this problem, one of the subgroups on the project isolated themselves from the rest of the team and worked intensely. They completed an essential piece of the software code, which got the project back on track, boosted moral, and allowed the product to be completed on time.

Companies such as Microsoft put processes in place that are scalable; that is, they have to work for large groups across a big organization. But sometimes scalable processes are not necessarily efficient. When there is a fire drill and things have to get done quickly, like with Tricia and the Zune team at Microsoft, companies need to break free of the bureaucracy. In fact, many companies decide to set up Skunk Works projects to do just this: they pull a team out of the normal workflow, giving them permission to break the rules, to free them to think and work differently.

Rules are often meant to be broken. This idea is captured in the oft-used phrase "Don't ask for permission, but beg for forgiveness." Most rules are in place as the lowest common denominator, making sure that those who don't have a clue what to do stay within the boundaries. If you ask someone how to go about making a movie, starting a company, getting into graduate school, or running for political office, you will usually get a long recipe that involves getting incrementally more support from those who are already in these fields. It involves agents and seed funding and exams and approvals. The majority of people choose to follow those rules . . . and others don't. It is important to keep in mind that there are often creative ways to work around the rules, to jump over the traditional hurdles, and to get to your goal by taking a side route. Just as most people wait in a never-ending line of traffic on the main route to the highway, others who are more adventurous try to find a side road to get to their destination more quickly. Of course, some rules are in place to protect our safety, to keep order, and to create a process that works for a large number of people. But it is worth questioning rules along the way. Sometimes side roads around the rules can get you to your goal even when the traditional paths appear blocked.

Linda Rottenberg, of Endeavor, shared a relevant story that had been passed on to her by one of her advisors, about two student fighter pilots who got together to share what they had learned from their respective instructors. The first pilot said, "I was given a thousand rules for flying my plane." The second pilot said, "I was only given three rules." The first pilot gloated, thinking he was given many more options, until his friend said, "My instructor told me the three things I should *never* do. All else is up to me." This story captures the idea that it is better to know the few things that are really against the rules than to focus on the many things you think you should do. This is also a reminder of the big difference between rules and recommendations. Once you whittle away the recommendations, there are often many fewer rules than you imagined. This is how Linda leads Endeavor: each franchise is given three things they can't do—the rest is completely up to them.

Another way to break the rules is to break free of expectations you have for yourself and that others have for you. Armen Berjikly, a computer scientist, always expected that he would spend his career working for a high technology company. He studied computer science as an undergraduate and management science as a graduate student. After completing school, he took a job as a product manager at a company called Echelon. Everything was going smoothly, he was well respected in the company, and his path was set. However, a close friend developed multiple sclerosis. He was so moved by her condition that he wanted to do whatever he could to help. In his free time after work and on weekends, he built a Web site called "This Is MS." The site offered useful information about MS and its treatments, and provided a confidential forum for people with MS to share their experiences. The site quickly gained traction because visitors were hungry for the chance to tell their stories. Armen realized he had struck a nerve. He decided to build an even bigger Web site that allowed anyone to share his or her experiences anonymously. This new site, called "The Experience Project," gained avid users quickly. Armen had to make a tough decision: Should he stay in the secure job with a reliable salary and a clear career path, or jump into the unknown by deciding to run The Experience Project full-time?

After serious consideration, Armen decided to break free from the expectations that both he and his family had for him in order to pursue this venture. It was a terribly hard choice, but it has been several years now and Armen doesn't regret his decision for a minute. The business is hard work, but the most challenging part was deciding to completely reinvent himself.[5]

So, let's step out of the high technology business world and see how you can break rules in order to create something of great value in a completely different arena. The past few years have seen growing interest in restaurants that look at food, cooking, and dining in a brand-new way. Instead of using traditional cooking techniques, a handful of chefs are experimenting with "molecular gastronomy," which involves stretching the limits of cooking in all sorts of unusual directions. These restaurants use equipment and materials straight out of a laboratory and play with your senses in wild ways. At Moto, in Chicago,[6] the kitchen is stocked with balloons, syringes, and dry ice, and the goal is to create food that is shocking yet tasty. They have a "tasting menu," where you actually eat the menu, which might, for example, taste like an Italian panini sandwich. Moto strives to break the rules with each dish they serve, from "delivering" food that looks like packing peanuts to the table in FedEx boxes to making a dessert that looks like nachos but is really made up of chocolate, frozen shredded mango, and cheesecake. Each dish is designed to push the boundary of how you imagine food should look and taste as they "transmogrify" your food into surprising shapes and forms. One of their chefs, Ben Roche, says their goal is to create a circus for your senses. They question every assumption about food preparation and presentation, develop brand-new cooking techniques, and even design custom utensils that are used to consume the food. This is a great reminder that in any arena, from your kitchen to your career, you can break free of the constraints that might be comfortable but are often limiting.

I met with a dozen current and former students, and asked them to share their stories about breaking free from expectations. After listening to all their tales about getting around obstacles in school, in the workplace, and when traveling, Mike Rothenberg, who graduated two years ago, summarized all he heard by stating, "All the cool stuff happens when you do things that are not the automatic next step." The well-worn path is there for everyone to trample. But the interesting things often occur when you are open to taking an unexpected turn, to trying something different, and when you are willing to question the rules others have made for you. All agreed that it is easy to stay on the prescribed path, but it is often much more interesting to discover the world of surprises lurking just around the corner.

Knowing that you can question the rules is terrifically empowering. It is a reminder that the traditional path is only one option available to you. You can always follow a recipe, drive on the major thoroughfares, and walk in the footsteps of those before you. But there are boundless additional options to explore if you are willing to identify and challenge assumptions, and to break free of the expectations that you and others project onto you. Don't be afraid to get out of your comfort zone, to have a healthy disregard for the impossible, and to turn well-worn ideas on their heads. As the students described above learned, it takes practice to do things that are not the "automatic next step." The more you experiment, the more you see that the spectrum of options is much broader than imagined. The sole rule is that you are limited only by your energy and imagination.

Chapter 4

PLEASE TAKE OUT YOUR WALLETS

Before retiring, my father was a successful corporate executive. He rose up through the ranks, from young engineer to manager to executive, and had senior roles at several large multinational companies. Growing up, I got used to learning that he had received promotions, from vice president to executive vice president to senior executive vice president, and so on. It happened like clockwork every two years or so. I was always impressed by my father's accomplishments and viewed him as a wonderful role model.

That said, I couldn't have been more surprised when my father got annoyed with me after I showed him one of my new business cards. They read "Tina L. Seelig, President." I had started my own venture and printed my own business cards. My father looked at the cards and then at me and said, "You can't just call yourself president." In his experience, you had to wait for someone else to promote you to a leadership role. You couldn't appoint yourself. He was so steeped in a world where others promote you to positions with greater responsibility that the thought of my anointing myself with that title perturbed him.

I have come across this mentality time and again. For example, twenty years ago when I told a friend I was going to write a book, she asked, "What makes you think you can write a book?" She couldn't imagine taking on such a project without the blessing of someone in a position of greater authority. I, on the other hand, felt confident I could do it. The task was certainly ambitious, but why not try? At the time there weren't any popular books on the chemistry of cooking. I wanted to read such a book, and since there wasn't one available, I decided to write one myself. I wasn't an expert on the topic, but as a scientist, figured I could learn the material along the way. I put together a detailed proposal, wrote some sample chapters, shopped it around, and landed a contract.

After my first book came out, I was surprised by how little promotion my publisher did, and decided to start a business to help authors get more exposure for their work and to help readers learn about books that might interest them. Again, quite a number of people asked me what made me think I could start a company. This was clearly a stretch for me, but I assumed I could figure it out. I started BookBrowser in 1991, several years before the Web was born. The idea was to create a kiosk-based system for bookstore customers that would "Match Books with Buys." I built the prototype on my Mac computer using HyperCard, a program that allowed users to put links from one "card" to another "card," just like HotLinks on the Web today. The software allowed users to follow links for a particular author, title, or genre. I also met with local bookstore managers, who agreed to put the kiosks in their stores, and I talked with dozens of publishers who were enthusiastic about including their books in the system. Satisfied that the idea was sound, I hired a team of programmers to implement the product. Nobody told me I could or should do this . . . I just did it.

Over time, I've became increasingly aware that the world is divided into people who wait for others to give them permission to do the things they want to do and people who grant themselves permission. Some look inside themselves for motivation and others wait to be pushed forward by outside forces. From my experience, there's a lot to be said for seizing opportunities instead of waiting for someone to hand them to you. There are always white spaces ready to be filled and golden nuggets of opportunities lying on the ground waiting for someone to pick them up. Sometimes it means looking beyond your own desk, outside your building, across the street, or around the corner. But the nuggets are there for the taking by anyone willing to gather them up.

This is exactly what Paul Yock discovered. Paul, as previously introduced, is the director of Stanford's BioDesign Program. His home base is the medical school, which is literally across the street from the engineering school. About ten years ago, Paul realized that Stanford was missing a huge opportunity by not finding ways for the medical school students and faculty to work with the engineering school students and faculty to invent new medical technologies. The medical folks, including doctors, students, and research scientists, needed engineers to design new products and processes to improve patient care; and the engineers across the street were looking for compelling problems to solve using their skills. Over the course of months, the various stakeholders met to discuss ways that they could work together. It was a complicated process since the two groups work so differently and have quite different vocabularies. Eventually, they hammered out a plan and the BioDesign Program was born. During the same time period, other colleagues in different medical and technical disciplines developed similar partnerships and the groups were gathered under one large umbrella, known as BioX. The idea was so big that it took several years to implement and resulted in productive cross-disciplinary collaboration and a stunning new building that now stands between the medical school and the engineering school. This story illustrates the fact that sometimes opportunities can be found right across the street—you just have to look up from your desk to see them. Nobody told Paul to do this. But he saw the need and filled it.

I've talked with many other people who have found constructive ways to bridge gaps and fill holes that others merely walk around, and in the process have anointed themselves to roles others might not have chosen for them. A wonderful example is Debra Dunn,[1] who spent a good part of her career at Hewlett-Packard. Her first job with HP was in the corporate headquarters. After several years she was strongly encouraged to take on a role within one of the operating units of the company, which would give her a better understanding of the inner workings of the organization. A position in human resources opened up in the test and measurement group. Although Debra didn't see herself as a career human resources manager, she decided to take the job because it would give her a chance to get an in-depth look at the functioning of an operating unit of the company.

After a couple of years, HP offered early retirement across the entire company as a way to avoid layoffs. With this incentive, the entire management team of her group decided to leave. The charter of the group changed completely, and a new general manager was brought in. There were some big holes to fill. Debra looked at the voids in the organization and decided to seize that opportunity. She volunteered to run all of manufacturing for the newly configured division. She'd never run a manufacturing group before, but having spent so much time working with the prior manufacturing directors, she was confident she could do it, and knew she could fill in her gaps of knowledge along the way. She was certainly not the typical candidate for the position, but she successfully convinced her new boss she could retool. In the end, Debra brought in a fresh perspective and was able to make many positive changes in the group. After only two years, she used the same strategy to move into a senior marketing job at HP. Again, Debra didn't wait for someone to tap her for the post; she simply figured out how to repackage her skills for the new position.

As demonstrated by Debra's story, one of the best ways to move from one field to another is to figure out how your skills can be translated into different settings. Others might not see the parallels on the surface, so it's your job to expose them. Sometimes the vocabulary in two disparate fields is completely different, but the job functions are remarkably similar. Consider the similarities between being a scientist and a management consultant: soon after earning my PhD in neuroscience, my sights were set on working in a startup biotechnology company. The only problem? I wanted a job in marketing and strategy, not in the lab. This seemed nearly impossible without any relevant experience. The startup companies with whom I interviewed were looking for individuals who could hit the ground running. I interviewed for months and months and often got close to a job offer, but nothing came through.

Eventually, I got an introduction to the managing director of the San Francisco branch of Booz Allen Hamilton, an international consulting company. My goal was to impress him enough that he would introduce me to some of the company's life science clients. I walked into the meeting and he asked me why someone with a PhD in neuroscience would be a good management consultant. I could have told him the truth—that I actually hadn't considered that option. But on the spot, with nothing to lose, I outlined the similarities between brain research and management consulting. For example, in both cases you need to identify the burning questions, collect relevant data, analyze it, select the most interesting results, craft a compelling presentation, and determine the next set of burning questions. He arranged other interviews for later that day, and I walked out that evening with a job offer. Of course, I took it. In fact, it turned out to be an amazing way to learn about business and a wide range of industries, and I certainly did leverage my prior training as a scientist. Out of necessity and curiosity, I've done this again and again, constantly reframing my skills to create new opportunities. When people ask me how a neuroscientist ended up teaching entrepreneurship to engineers, I have to say, "It's a long story."

All of these cases illustrate that in any complex organization, there are always opportunities around you. Even if tackling them doesn't seem like a natural fit for you, with a little bit of creativity, you can usually find a way that your skills are relevant to the challenge. Paul Yock identified a missed opportunity in a university setting and designed a brand-new program to fill the need; Debra Dunn saw holes in her organization and found a way to leverage what she knew to take on roles others would not necessarily have chosen for her; and I figured out a creative way to reframe my skills so I could move between two fields that on the surface looked completely disparate.

• • •

Another way to anoint yourself is to look at things others have discarded and find ways to turn them into something useful. There is often tremendous value in the projects others have carelessly abandoned. As discussed previously, sometimes people jettison ideas because they don't fully appreciate their value, or because they don't have time to fully explore them. Often these discarded ideas hold a lot of promise.

Michael Dearing started his career in strategy at Disney, went on to launch a retail venture that failed, and then landed at eBay, a leading online auction Web site. Michael was initially assigned to a job he wasn't thrilled about. He decided to use his free time to look at features that had been designed but then ignored or abandoned, ideas just waiting for someone to exploit them. It was the year 2000, and Michael saw that there was a new feature that let customers add a photo to their standard listing for an additional twenty-five cents. Only 10 percent of eBay customers were using this feature. Michael spent some time analyzing the benefits of this service and was able to demonstrate that products with accompanying photos sold faster and at a higher price than products without photos. Armed with this compelling data, he started marketing the photo service more heavily and ended up increasing the adoption rate of this feature by customers from 10 percent to 60 percent. This resulted in $300 million in additional annual revenue for eBay. Without any instructions from others, Michael found an untapped gold mine and exploited it with great results. The cost to the company was minimal and the profits were profound.

This wasn't the first time Michael found a way to tap into resources around him. Even as a kid he wrote letters to famous people and was pleased to see that most of the time they wrote back. He still continues that habit, sending unsolicited e-mails to people he admires. In almost every instance they respond, and in many cases the correspondence results in long-term relationships and interesting opportunities. He never asks the folks he writes for anything. His initial contact is all about thanking them for something they've done, acknowledging something they've accomplished, asking a simple question, or offering to help them in some way. He doesn't wait for an invitation to contact these people, but takes it upon himself to make the first move.

There is considerable research showing that those willing to stretch the boundaries of their current skills and willing to risk trying something new, like Debra Dunn and Michael Dearing, are much more likely to be successful than those who believe they have a fixed skill set and innate abilities that lock them into specific roles. Carol Dweck, at Stanford's psychology department, has written extensively about this, demonstrating that those of us with a fixed mind-set about what we're good at are much less likely to be successful in the long run than those with a growth mind-set. Her work focuses on our attitude about ourselves. Those with a fixed image about what they can do are much less likely to take risks that might shake that image. But those with a growth mind-set are typically open to taking risks and tend to work harder to reach their objectives. They're willing to try new things that push their abilities, opening up entirely new arenas along the way.

So how do you find holes that need to be filled? It's actually quite simple. The first step is learning how to pay attention. My colleagues at the d.school developed the following exercise, which gets at the heart of identifying opportunities. Participants are asked to take out their wallets. They then break up into pairs and interview one another about their wallets. They discuss what they love and hate about their wallets, paying particular attention to how they use them for purchasing and storage.

One of the most interesting insights comes from watching each person pull out his or her wallet at the beginning. Some of the wallets are trim and neat, some are practically exploding with papers, some are fashion statements, some carry the individual's entire library of photos and receipts, and some consist of little more than a paper clip. Clearly, a wallet plays a different role for each of us. The interview process exposes how each person uses his or her wallet, what it represents, and the strange behaviors each has developed to get around the wallet's limitations. I've never seen a person who is completely satisfied with his or her wallet: there is always something that can be fixed. In fact, most people are walking around with wallets that drive them crazy in some way. They discuss their frustrations with the size of their wallets, their inability to find things easily, or their desire to have different types of wallets for different occasions.

After the interview process, each person designs and builds a new wallet for the other person—his or her "customer." The design materials include nothing more than paper, tape, markers, scissors, paper clips, and the like. They can also use whatever else they find in the room. This takes about thirty minutes. After they've completed the prototype, they "sell" it to their customer. Almost universally, the new wallet solves the biggest problems with which the customer was struggling. They're thrilled with the concept and say that if that wallet were available, they would buy it. Some of the features are based on science fiction, such as a wallet that prints money on demand, but some require little more than a good designer to make them feasible right away.

Many lessons fall out of this exercise. First, the wallet is symbolic of the fact that problems are everywhere, even in your back pocket. Second, it doesn't take much effort to uncover these problems. In fact, people are generally happy to tell you about their problems. Third, by experimenting, you get quick and dirty feedback on the solutions you propose. It doesn't take much work, many resources, or much time. And, finally, if you aren't on the right track with a solution, the sunk cost is really low. All you have to do is start over.[2]

I've run this exercise with small groups, with large groups, with kids, with doctors, and with business executives. In all cases they're surprised by the simplicity of realizing that there are always things that can be improved—from wallets and shoelaces to backpacks, software, restaurants, gas stations, cars, clothes, coffee shops . . . the list is endless. You don't need someone else to give you this assignment. In fact, all successful entrepreneurs do this naturally. They pay attention at home, at work, at the grocery store, in airplanes, at the beach, at the doctor's office, or on the baseball field, and find an array of opportunities to fix things that are broken.

The wallet design exercise focuses on product design. But you can use the same approach to rethink services, experiences, and organization structures. At the d.school, the teaching team crafts projects that charge the students with completely rethinking an amazingly wide range of experiences, from primary school education in the United States to irrigation of crops in rural India and management of innovative organizations. If you study each situation with an eye for improvement, you will find countless opportunities. It is then up to you to decide if you will put yourself in the position to take on that challenge.

Some people are masters at taking on challenges and seizing leadership roles. I learned a lot about this from David Rothkopf, author and CEO of Garten Rothkopf, a Washington, DC–based international advisory firm, whose book *Superclass* focuses on those people in the world who have more power and influence than the rest of us.[3] David studied leaders who've made it to the inner circle, interacting with one another in the elite World Economic Forum that meets annually in Davos, Switzerland. I asked David what sets these people apart from the rest of us. He echoed many of the things that others in this book mentioned: people who get to the top work harder than those around them, they have more energy that propels them forward, and they're markedly more driven to get there. He notes that in the past people in the inner circle inherited their wealth and access. But today that isn't the case. The majority of people who claim great success have made it happen on their own. This means that the primary barriers to success are self-imposed. The corollary to this is, as David says, "The biggest ally of superachievers is the inertia of others."

David actually embodies these characteristics himself, naturally seizing opportunities, as opposed to waiting for others to hand them to him. His first company was called International Media Partners, and one of their activities was organizing conferences for top CEOs. The looming question for this startup was how to get all those exclusive and elusive executives in the same room. David and his partners needed a tempting hook, and decided that getting Henry Kissinger to speak would do the trick. But how would they get Henry Kissinger to participate? David found out how to reach Kissinger's office and asked Kissinger's staff if he was available to speak at the conference. No problem . . . but it would cost $50,000, require a private airplane with two pilots, and a chauffeured limousine. David and his team didn't have any money, so any amount was too much . . . but he said, "Yes, we'll do it." He assumed that if he could get Henry Kissinger in the room, then the rest would fall neatly into place—and it did! Once Kissinger accepted, they were able to secure Alexander Haig, Secretary of State under President Reagan; then Edmund Muskie, Secretary of State under Jimmy Carter; followed by a long list of other well-known speakers. With this list of luminaries, the CEOs showed up in droves and the company was able to get sponsors who more than paid for all the speaking fees. The fact that David didn't know Henry Kissinger and had no money didn't get in his way. He succeeded by creatively leveraging what he did have—his energy, his willingness to work hard, and his drive to make it happen.

The story goes on from here. David's colleague at International Media Partners, Jeffrey Garten, went on to become Undersecretary of Commerce during the first Clinton administration. He invited David to become Deputy Undersecretary of Commerce for International Trade. It seemed like a pretty plum position. He had a huge office and a big staff. But after two weeks David walked into Jeff's office and quit. He couldn't stand the bureaucratic environment. Everything was painfully slow and David was impatient to make things happen. Jeff took David outside for a walk and told him the following joke:

> There was once a man named Goldberg who wanted nothing more than to be rich. So each day he went the synagogue and prayed to God to win the lottery. This went on for days, weeks, months, and years, but Goldberg

never won. Eventually, Goldberg was at his wit's end. Praying to God, he said, "You have really let me down." Suddenly the silence was broken and God responded in a booming voice, "Goldberg, you've got to help me out here. You could at least buy a ticket!"

Jeff reminded David of something he already knew—he wasn't going to "win the lottery" in Washington if he didn't engage. Nobody was going to hand him the tools to be successful. So David went back to his office and tapped into his natural instincts to make things happen, as opposed to waiting for someone to show up with a game plan. He quickly realized that there were endless holes to be filled and tremendous resources at his disposal. In a wonderful finale, several years after David left the Department of Commerce he became the managing director of Kissinger Associates, Inc. He went from being a newcomer who dreamed of being in the same room with Henry Kissinger to joining him as a business partner.

David has seen this story play out again and again in his own life and in the lives of those he has studied while researching his book. Those who are successful find ways to make themselves successful. There is no recipe, no secret handshake, and no magic potion. Each person he studied has a story as unique as a fingerprint. The consistent theme is that they each pay attention to current trends and leverage their own skills to build their influence. They find ways to sway history, as opposed to waiting for history to sway them.

If you want a leadership role, then take on leadership roles. Just give yourself permission to do so. Look around for holes in your organization, ask for what you want, find ways to leverage your skills and experiences, be willing to make the first move, and stretch beyond what you've done before. There are always opportunities waiting to be exploited. Instead of waiting to be asked and tiptoeing around an opportunity, seize it. It takes hard work, energy, and drive—but these are the assets that set leaders apart from those who wait for others to anoint them.

Chapter 5

THE SECRET SAUCE OF SILICON VALLEY

I require my students to write a failure résumé. That is, to craft a résumé that summarizes all their biggest screwups—personal, professional, and academic. For every failure, each student must describe what he or she learned from that experience. Just imagine the looks of surprise this assignment inspires in students who are so used to showcasing their successes. However, after they finish their résumé, they realize that viewing experiences through the lens of failure forced them to come to terms with the mistakes they have made along the way. In fact, as the years go by, many former students continue to keep their failure résumé up-to-date, in parallel with their traditional résumé of successes.

I borrowed this assignment from Liz Kisenwether at Penn State University. When I first heard the idea I thought it was terrific. It's a quick way to demonstrate that failure is an important part of our learning process, especially when you're stretching your abilities, doing things the first time, or taking risks. We hire people who have experience not just because of their successes but also because of their failures. Failures offer learning opportunities and increase the chance that you won't make the same mistake again. Failures are also a sign that you have taken on challenges that expand your skills. In fact, many successful people believe that if you aren't failing sometimes then you aren't taking enough risks. Prodded by a former student, I decided to include here my own abbreviated failure résumé, showcasing some of my biggest mistakes. I wish I had kept this résumé up-to-date for the past thirty years. It would have been fascinating to revisit and learn from all the mistakes I've conveniently put out of my mind.

TINA L. SEELIG

Professional Failures

Not paying attention: Early in my career I naively thought I knew how organizations worked. I made judgments about corporate culture that were incorrect. I wish I had spent more time paying attention and less time making assumptions.

Quitting too early: While running my own business I hit the wall. It got incredibly hard both technically and organizationally, and was going to take a tremendous amount of effort to find my way to a solution. I wish I had been confident enough to fully commit to finding a solution.

Academic Failures

Not doing my best: The first two years of college I didn't put my focused effort into all my courses. I missed the chance to extract the most value from the classes—a chance I can't get back.

Relationship management: I had a challenging relationship with my PhD advisor. I wanted to spend a lot of time teaching and she felt I should spend most of my time in the lab. I wish I had found a way to better align our goals.

Personal Failures

Avoiding conflicts: I had a boyfriend in college, and as we closed in on graduation we were both stressed about where we were going next. Instead of dealing with the questions directly, I blew up the relationship. I wish I had been able to talk honestly about what was going on.

Not listening to my gut: My uncle died in New York. I lived in California and several people urged me not to travel to the funeral. I have always regretted it. I learned that there are some things you can't undo, and that in situations such as these I should do what is right for me, not necessarily what others want me to do.

• • •

Willingness to take risks and reactions to failure differ dramatically around the world. In some cultures the downside for failure is so high that individuals are allergic to taking any risks at all. These cultures associate shame with any type of failure, and from a young age people are taught to follow a prescribed path with a well-defined chance of success, as opposed to trying anything that might lead to disappointment. In some places, such as Thailand, someone who has failed repeatedly might even choose to take on a brand-new name in an attempt to reboot his or her entire life. In fact, in the 2008 Olympics, a Thai weight lifter attributed her victory to changing her name before the games.

The Global Entrepreneurship Monitor (GEM),[1] which publishes a detailed annual report on startup activity around the world, looks at cultural differences in risk taking and comfort with failure. The GEM team found that important factors contribute to a society's risk profile. For example, in some countries, such as Sweden, the bankruptcy laws are designed such that once your company goes out of business you can never get out of debt. Knowing that failure has drastic, long-term consequences for you and your family is a huge disincentive to try to start a company in the first place. The culture in other countries is equally unforgiving. Once you fail, your friends, neighbors, and colleagues will always view you as a failure. A recent issue of the *Wall Street Journal* describes humiliating tactics currently used by debt collectors in several countries, including Spain.[2] The collectors literally show up at individuals' houses in bizarre costumes, with the goal of drawing attention from the neighbors and shaming the debtors. Why would anyone in these communities risk public ridicule by taking on any unnecessary risk?

This is in sharp contrast to Silicon Valley, where failure is acknowledged as a natural part of the process of innovation. Steve Jurvetson,[3] a partner at the venture firm Draper Fisher Jurvetson, describes failure as the secret sauce of Silicon Valley, while Randy Komisar of KPCB notes that being able to view failure as an asset is the hallmark of an entrepreneurial environment. Randy also says that when he sees people who have never had a failure, he wonders what they have really learned from their experiences.

On the most basic level, all learning comes from failure. Think of a baby learning to walk. He or she starts out crawling and then falling before finally mastering the skill that as an adult we take for granted. As a child gets older, each new feat, from catching a baseball to doing algebra, is learned the same way, by experimenting until you are finally successful. We don't expect a child to do everything perfectly the first time, nor should we expect adults who take on complex tasks to get it all right the first time, either.

I've come to believe that the most powerful learning comes from experiencing failures as well as successes. It is also nearly impossible to learn anything without doing it yourself, by experimenting along the way, and by recovering from the inevitable failures. You can't learn to play soccer by reading the rulebook, you can't learn to play the piano by studying sheets of music, and you can't learn to cook by reading recipes. I'm reminded of my time as a graduate student in neuroscience. I had taken several courses in which we "learned" the principles of neurophysiology. Although I could pass a written test on the material, it wasn't until I was in the lab, dissecting nerves under a microscope, impaling them with tiny electrodes, and manually turning the dials on the oscilloscope, that I fully understood the concepts. Likewise, you can read as many books on leadership as you want, but until you experience the challenges that face real leaders, you will never be prepared to take charge.

The Mayfield Fellows Program, which I co-direct with Tom Byers, a professor in Management Science and Engineering at Stanford, gives students this opportunity.[4] After one quarter of classroom work, during which we offer an in-depth introduction to entrepreneurship through case studies, the twelve students in this nine-month program spend the summer working in startup companies. They take on key roles in each business and are closely mentored by senior leaders in the company. They experience firsthand what it is like to identify and address the white-hot risks that face each organization, the stresses of making decisions with incomplete information, and the challenge of leading in an ever-changing environment. After the intense summer experience, the students come back to class for ten weeks of debriefing about what happened in their respective companies. Each student leads a class on an important issue that evolved during their internship.

The students in the Mayfield Fellows Program have profound insights about what it means to run a fast-paced business in a dynamic environment. They watch these companies struggle with issues such as running out of cash, retooling after a change in the senior management team, the challenge of getting cutting-edge technology to work, and the daunting task of competing against giants in the industry. By the end of the summer, the students realize that only a handful of the companies for which they worked will be in business in a year or two. Despite all of the efforts of talented teams, many of them will fail.

The entire venture capital industry essentially invests in failures, since the majority of the companies they fund eventually go under. Other industries have a similar success rate, including the toy industry, the movie business, and the publishing industry. Consider book publishing: According to Nielsen Bookscan, of the approximately 1.2 million different books in print in 2004, only 25,000, or 2 percent, sold more than 5,000 copies, and the average book in the U.S., sells less than 500 copies. However, it is nearly impossible to predict which ones will be the big hits. As a result, publishers continue to produce many different books, hoping that each will be a success but knowing that only a tiny fraction will make it onto the bestseller list. Publishers, toy makers, movie producers, and venture capitalists understand that the path to success is littered with failures.

Mir Imran, a serial entrepreneur, has started dozens of companies, many in parallel.[5] His success rate has been remarkable, considering that in almost every environment most startups fail. When asked about his success rate, Mir admits that the key is killing projects early. He uses a brutal process to weed out projects with a low likelihood of success and puts increased energy into those with a high likelihood of making it to the finish line. He uses considerable discipline and analysis in the early stages, prior to launching a new venture, to increase the chances that it will thrive in the long run.

Even though it is always difficult to abandon a project, it is much easier in the early stages of a venture, before there is an enormous escalation of committed time and energy. This happens in all parts of our lives, including jobs, stock investments, and any type of relationship. Leonardo da Vinci once stated, "It is easier to resist at the beginning than at the end." Bob Sutton, an expert on organizational behavior, describes "The Da Vinci Rule" in detail in his book, *The No Asshole Rule,* where he talks about leaving jobs that are not a good match as soon as you discover they are untenable.[6] Here he generalizes this much more broadly:

> Although most people know that sunk costs shouldn't be considered in making a decision, the "too-much-

> invested-to-quit syndrome" is a powerful driver of human behavior. We justify all the time, effort, suffering, and years and years that we devote to something by telling ourselves and others that there must be something worthwhile and important about it or we never would have sunk so much of our lives into it.

Quitting is actually incredibly empowering. It's a reminder that you control the situation and can leave whenever you like. You don't have to be your own prison guard, keeping yourself locked up in a place that isn't working. But that doesn't mean quitting is easy. I've quit jobs that were a bad match and abandoned failing projects, and in each case it was terribly difficult. We're taught that quitting is a sign of weakness, although in many circumstances, it's just the opposite. Sometimes quitting is the bravest alternative, because it requires you to face your failures and announce them publicly. The great news is that quitting allows you to start over with a clean slate. And, if you take the time to evaluate what happened, quitting can be an invaluable learning experience.

When Randy Komisar left his vice president position at Claris, a computer software company that spun out of Apple Computer, he felt he had failed. Randy, who had a clear vision of what he wanted to accomplish, left Claris when he realized he was never going to achieve his goals. Randy's "failure" was very public, and it stung badly. However, within a short time Randy realized that being released from this job provided him with an opportunity to reevaluate his passions and determine how he could best use his skills. For instance, it became clear that one reason he felt so dissatisfied at Claris was that he was neither passionate about the product nor about what he was doing. He loved thinking about the company's big picture and scoping out its vision, but he was hardly inspired by the day-to-day management issues.

When Randy was asked to become CEO of a new company, he suggested instead that he work *with* the CEO to set the direction for the company. In this way he crafted a brand-new role for himself—"Virtual CEO"—and was subsequently able to become involved with dozens of companies, many at the same time. He served as a coach, sounding board, and advisor for CEOs, but didn't have the day-to-day responsibilities. This suited him and the companies well. "The failure allowed me to better align my passions with the opportunities around me," says Randy. This is a poignant reminder that learning when to call it quits is crucial. You need to know when to stop pounding on an idea that isn't working and when to move on to something new.

There are actually many ways to turn a failure into a success. One memorable story about transforming a big disappointment into a big win came out of the Innovation Tournament in which students had to create value from rubber bands in five days. One team decided to create a "Wishing Tree." They identified a tree in the center of campus, across from the university bookstore, and wrapped the trunk with chicken wire. They then used rubber bands to attach messages to the chicken wire. The idea was that anyone passing by could post a wish on the tree. The team promoted it widely, using online networking sites, e-mail lists, and by literally standing in front of the tree, inviting passersby to post a wish. Unfortunately, people just weren't interested.

In an attempt to build momentum, the team started seeding the tree with wishes. This had little affect. They then became more aggressive in their promotion and more actively invited passersby to contribute. Again, this had little impact. But the students' disappointment was amplified by the fact that not more than fifty feet away a similar project was getting lots of attention. Another team had created a huge web of large rubber bands from which they invited students to suspend their secrets. The rubber-band web was brimming with hundreds of brightly colored papers, each with a different secret. They fluttered in the light breeze, in sharp contrast to the nearly naked Wishing Tree next door.

The Wishing Tree team decided to chalk this one up as a failure. However, they didn't stop there. They extracted as much as they could from this experience by making a provocative three-minute video documenting the failure. The team described all of their attempts to make the Wishing Tree successful and compared their failure to the success of the "Web of Secrets." They very publicly celebrated their failure and shared what they had learned about the "stickiness" of wishes versus secrets. (Stories, products, and Web sites are "sticky" when they hold your attention and don't let go.) They also made it clear that this was just one step along the path to the next idea, and the next, and the next.

Because even great ideas require a tremendous amount of work to reach a successful outcome, it's incredibly hard to know when to keep pushing on a problem, hoping for a breakthrough, and when to walk away. We all know that persistence is to be admired, but when does it become foolish to continue working on something that's never going to fly? Gil Penchina, CEO of Wikia, describes the dilemma wonderfully: "If you throw gasoline on a log, all you get is a wet log. But if you throw gasoline on a small flame, you get an inferno."[7] That is, it's important to know whether you're putting energy into something that has the potential to pay off. This is one of life's biggest challenges. We often stay in dead-end situations way too long. This occurs when companies commit to a doomed product or project, or when individuals stay with jobs or in relationships that make them miserable, hoping the situation will improve.

So how do you know when to quit? This is a huge philosophical question. It's always a mammoth challenge to separate your desire to make something work from the reality of the probability that it will work. Of course, the more you put into a project, the more likely it is to succeed. But some efforts will never pan out, no matter how much time, money, or sweat is injected. The most scientific answer I've found is, listen to your gut and look at your alternatives. Essentially, you have to negotiate honestly with yourself. Do you have the fortitude to push through the problems in front of you to reach a successful outcome, or are you better off taking another path?

So quitting is hard—but it's even harder to do it well. I've seen people quit gracefully and others quit so clumsily that they leave a huge crater in their wake. As discussed in detail in chapter 8, you are likely to bump into the same people again and again in life, often in unexpected ways. This alone is reason enough to make sure that when you quit, you do so with careful thought about the consequences for those around you. Besides the impact that quitting gracefully might have on you later, it is just the right thing to do. You can never rationalize quitting in such a way that you hurt your colleagues, friends, or former business.

A colleague told me about his assistant, who was doing a terrific job. He gave her great reviews and spent a lot of time talking with her about her career path within his group. She made it clear that ultimately she hoped to move into a different field, and my colleague was supportive of this. In fact, he told her he would be delighted to serve as a reference for her anytime. With this as a backdrop, my colleague couldn't have been more surprised when his assistant came in one day and gave two weeks' notice. The team was in the midst of a huge project, the deadline three weeks away. She was going to leave one week before the project was completed, putting the entire team in a very difficult position. My colleague asked her several times if she would consider staying one more week to help him get to the end of the project, which involved dozens of people directly and several thousands indirectly. She refused, saying, "I know you're going to be unhappy that I'm leaving no matter when I go, so I decided to do what I want." My colleague felt as though he'd been kicked in the stomach. It was nearly impossible to fill in the holes she left during the last week of the project, and everyone worked around the clock to try to fill the void. All those who worked with her will remember that decision. Despite the fact that she did a terrific job while she was with them, the damage she did to her reputation during the last weeks of her employment dwarfed all the positive things she had done in prior years.

In sharp contrast, I've seen others quit jobs with remarkable style. Even if they were leaving because the job wasn't a good match, the grace with which they left made such a positive impression that everyone involved would be pleased to give them a glowing recommendation at any time in the future. They provided enough notice to fill any gaps, they took the time to put their work in order so that someone else could pick up where they left off, and they even offered to help with the transition. These folks are heroes. They mastered the art of quitting well, and used their skill to turn a bad situation into something positive.

So how do you prepare yourself for inevitable failures? People who spend their time on creative endeavors know that failure is a natural part of the creative process and are ready when it happens. Jeff Hawkins gets worried when things go too smoothly, knowing that failure must be lurking around the corner. When he was running Handspring, everything was going swimmingly for the release of the original "Visor", a new personal digital assistant. But Jeff kept warning his team that something would happen. And it did. Within the first few days of the release of their first product they shipped about 100,000 units. This was remarkable. But the entire billing and shipping system broke down. Some customers didn't receive the products they paid for, and others received three or four times as many units as they ordered. This was a disaster, especially for a new business that was trying to build its reputation. So what did they do? The entire team, including Jeff, buckled down and called each and every customer. They asked each person what he or she had ordered, if they had received it, and whether they had been billed correctly. If anything wasn't perfect, the company corrected it on the spot. The key point is that Jeff knew something would go wrong. He wasn't sure what it would be, but was prepared to deal with anything that came their way. His experience has taught him that failure is inevitable, and that the key to success is not dodging every bullet but being able to recover quickly.

This theme comes up again and again when listening to those who have been successful. They are willing to try lots of things, and are confident that some of their experiments will lead to great outcomes. But they also recognize that there will be potholes along the way. This approach can be used for big and small challenges. Consider the following story, told to me by a friend: There was a man who appeared to have endless luck with women. He wasn't particularly charming, funny, smart, or attractive, so it was quite a mystery. One day my friend asked him how he managed to have such a steady flow of women in his life. He confided that it was simple—he asked every attractive woman he met for a date, and some of them said yes. He was willing to take his share of rejections in return for a handful of successes. This brings the lesson to its basest level. If you get out there and try lots of things, you're much more likely to find success than someone who waits around for the phone to ring.

This story is consistent with advice my father always gave me: being a squeaky wheel rarely changes the outcome, but it does allow you to get to the conclusion sooner. Don't sit around waiting for a yes that will never come. It's better to get to no sooner rather than later, so you can put your energy into opportunities with a higher likelihood of success. This applies to job hunting, finding business funding, dating, and most other endeavors. That is, if you continue to push the limits, and are willing to fail along the way, you will very likely find success.

These stories highlight an important point: a successful career is not a straight line but a wave with ups and downs. Michael Dearing describes this wonderfully with a simple graph that maps a typical career, with *time* on the x-axis and *success* on the y-axis. Most people feel as though they should be constantly progressing up and to the right, moving along a straight success line. But this is both unrealistic and limiting. In reality, when you look closely at the graph for most successful people, there are always ups and downs. When viewed over a longer period of time, however, the line generally moves up and to the right. When you're in a down cycle, it's sometimes hard to see that the temporary dip is actually a setup for the next rise. In fact, the slope of the upward line is often steeper after a down cycle, meaning you're really achieving more than if you had stayed on a steady, predictable path.

Carol Bartz, the former CEO of Autodesk and new CEO of Yahoo!, uses another great analogy to describe a successful career path.[8] She thinks you should look at the progress of your career as moving around and up a three-dimensional pyramid, as opposed to up a two-dimensional ladder. Lateral moves along the side of the pyramid often allow you to build the base of your experience. It may not look as though you're moving up quickly, but you're gathering a foundation of skills and experiences that will prove extremely valuable later.

One of my favorite stories about the cyclical and unpredictable nature of careers comes from Steve Jobs. As the founder of Apple and Pixar, his success stories are legendary. However, many of his finest successes grew out of failures. He described these stories beautifully when he gave the commencement address at Stanford in 2005. Here is an excerpt of his speech:

We had just released our finest creation—the Macintosh—a year earlier, and I had just turned thirty. And then I got fired. How can you get fired from a company you started? Well, as Apple grew we hired someone who I thought was very talented to run the company with me, and for the first year or so things went well. But then our visions of the future began to diverge and eventually we had a falling out. When we did, our Board of Directors sided with him. So at thirty I was out. And very publicly out. What had been the focus of my entire adult life was gone, and it was devastating.

I really didn't know what to do for a few months. I felt that I had let the previous generation of entrepreneurs down—that I had dropped the baton as it was being passed to me. I met with David Packard and Bob Noyce and tried to apologize for screwing up so badly. I was a very public failure, and I even thought about running away from the Valley. But something slowly began to dawn on me—I still loved what I did. The turn of events at Apple had not changed that one bit. I had been rejected, but I was still in love. And so I decided to start over.

I didn't see it then, but it turned out that getting fired from Apple was the best thing that could have ever happened to me. The heaviness of being successful was replaced by the lightness of being a beginner again, less sure about everything. It freed me to enter one of the most creative periods of my life.

During the next five years, I started a company named NeXT, another company named Pixar, and fell in love with an amazing woman who would become my wife. Pixar went on to create the world's first computer-animated feature film, *Toy Story*, and is now the most successful animation studio in the world. In a remarkable turn of events, Apple bought NeXT, I returned to Apple, and the technology we developed at NeXT is at the heart of Apple's current renaissance. And Laurene and I have a wonderful family together.

I'm pretty sure none of this would have happened if I hadn't been fired from Apple. It was awful tasting medicine, but I guess the patient needed it. Sometimes life hits you in the head with a brick.

This story is echoed time and time again. Essentially, most individual's paths are riddled with small and enormous failures. The key is being able to recover from them. For most successful people, the bottom is lined with rubber as opposed to concrete. When they hit bottom, they sink in for a bit and then bounce back, tapping into the energy of the impact to propel them into another opportunity. A great example is David Neeleman, the founder of JetBlue.[9] David initially started an airline called Morris Air, which grew and prospered, and he sold it to Southwest Airlines for $130 million. He then became an employee of Southwest. After only five months David was fired. He was miserable working for them and, as he says, he was driving them crazy. As part of his contract he had a five-year noncompete agreement that prevented him from starting another airline. That seemed like a lifetime to wait. But after taking time to recover from this blow, David decided to spend that time planning for his next airline venture. He thought through all the details of the company, including the corporate values, the complete customer experience, the type of people they would hire, as well as the details of how they would train and compensate their employees. David says that getting fired and having to wait to start another airline was the best thing that ever happened to him. When the noncompete period was over, he was ready to hit the ground running. Just like Steve Jobs, he was able to turn what seemed like a terrible situation into a period of extreme productivity and creativity.

Failing, of course, isn't fun. It's much more fun to tell the world about our successes. But failures can serve as incredible opportunities in disguise. They force us to reevaluate our goals and priorities, and often propel us forward much faster than continued success.

Getting too comfortable with failure, however, seems risky. Are those who celebrate failure doomed to fail? Imagine corporate "Employee of the Month" photos showcasing the biggest screwups. However, as Bob Sutton points out in *Weird Ideas That Work*, rewarding only successes can stifle innovation because it discourages risk taking. Bob suggests that organizations consider rewarding successes *and* failures, and punishing inaction. Doing so would encourage people to experiment, which is more likely to lead to interesting and unexpected outcomes.

> I am not saying that your company should reward people who are stupid, lazy, or incompetent. I mean you should reward smart failures, not dumb failures. If you want a creative organization, inaction is the worst kind of failure. . . . Creativity results from action, rather than inaction, more than anything else.

Bob adds that there is strong evidence that the ratio between our individual successes and failures stays the same. Therefore, if you want more successes, you're going to have to be willing to live with more failures. Failure is the flip side of success, and you can't have one without the other.

At the d.school there is a lot of emphasis on taking big risks to earn big rewards. Students are encouraged to think really *big*, even if there's a significant chance that a project won't be successful. To encourage this, we reward spectacular disasters. Students are told that it is much better to have a flaming failure than a so-so success. Jim Plummer, the dean of Stanford's School of Engineering, embraces this philosophy. He tells his PhD students that they should pick a thesis project that has a 20 percent chance of success. Some students find this discouraging, interpreting this to mean that they will have to do five different projects before they reach completion. Quite the contrary. The experiments should be designed so that a failure is informative and a success leads to a major breakthrough. Doing small, incremental experiments with predictable results is much less valuable than taking a big risk that will potentially lead to a much bigger reward.

The flip side of being comfortable with failure, and walking away from a project that doesn't work, is the risk of quitting too early. Take the classic story of 3M's Post-it notes, which began with an adhesive that didn't stick and turned into a multibillion-dollar business. In 1968, Spencer Silver invented this "low tack" adhesive and promoted it internally at 3M, but initially no one was interested. It wasn't until 1974 that a colleague, Art Fry, realized he could use the substandard glue to keep bookmarks in place in his church hymnal and spent his free time designing the product we now know as Post-its. It wasn't until six years later that 3M launched the product across the United States. Today they sell more than six hundred Post-it products in more than a hundred countries. Imagine the lost opportunity if the engineers at 3M hadn't realized the potential in this "failed" product. This mind-set is captured in the class project discussed earlier, where teams turn bad ideas into great ideas.

We often live on the edge of success and failure, and it is rarely clear which way we will land. This uncertainty is amplified in high-risk ventures such as restaurants, technology startups, and even sports, where the line between success and failure may be razor thin. Consider the Tour de France. Even after days of cycling up and down steep and winding mountains, the time difference between the winners and the losers boils down to a matter of seconds, if not milliseconds. Sometimes a little extra push is all it takes to flip the switch from failure to success.

Some companies have mastered the ability to coax the value from products that others might discard as failures. Marissa Mayer, who leads product development at Google, says it is important not to kill projects too early, but to morph them instead.[10] That is, figure out what part is working well and what needs to be improved instead of discarding it. Marissa believes that there is usually a way to extract some value from any project, even one that doesn't seem to be working.

Google and other Web companies rely upon "A-B" testing. That is, they release two versions of the software at the same time and receive quick feedback on what approach is more successful. These companies find that by making small modifications, such as changing the color of a button, adding a single word to a message, or moving images around the page, they can dramatically alter a customer's response. Some Web-based businesses release dozens of versions of the same product a day, each altering the user experience in some small way so that they can evaluate the response.

A company founded by two former Stanford students, Jeff Seibert and Kimber Lockhart, uses this approach all the time. GetBackboard.com is a Web site for collecting feedback on documents. They continue to experiment with different "calls to action" on their Web site and keep track of which approach works best. When they had a green bubble that said "Get an Account Today," they had an 8 percent sign-up rate. When the message was changed to "Easy Quick Signup," the response rate increased to 11 percent. And when the text offered a "Free 30 Day Trial," the response jumped to 14 percent. This type of experimentation turns failures into successes, and makes successes more successful.

Trying new things requires a willingness to take risks. However, risk taking is not binary. I'd bet that you're comfortable taking some types of risks and find other types quite uncomfortable. You might not even see the risks that are comfortable for you to take, discounting their riskiness, but are likely to amplify the risk of things that make you more anxious. For example, you might love flying down a ski slope at lightning speed or jumping out of airplanes, and don't view these activities as risky. If so, you're blind to the fact that you're taking on significant physical risk. Others, like me, who are not physical risk takers, would rather sip hot chocolate in the ski lodge or buckle themselves tightly into their airplane seats than strap on a pair of ski boots or a parachute. Alternatively, you might feel perfectly comfortable with social risks, such as giving a speech to a large crowd. This doesn't seem risky at all to me. But others, who might be perfectly happy jumping out of a plane, would never give a toast at a party.

On reflection, there appear to be five primary types of risks: physical, social, emotional, financial, and intellectual. For example, I know that I'm comfortable taking social risks but not physical risks. In short, I will readily start a conversation with a stranger, but please don't ask me to bungee jump off a bridge. I will also happily take intellectual risks that stretch my analytical abilities, but I'm not a big financial risk taker. On a trip to Las Vegas I would bring only a small amount of cash, to make sure I didn't lose too much.

I often ask people to map their own risk profile. With only a little bit of reflection, each person knows which types of risks he or she is willing to take. They realize pretty quickly that risk taking isn't uniform. It's interesting to note that most entrepreneurs don't see themselves as big risk takers. After analyzing the landscape, building a great team, and putting together a detailed plan, they feel as though they have squeezed as much risk out of the venture as they can. In fact, they spend most of their efforts working to reduce the risks for their business.

Elisabeth Pate Cornell, chair of the Department of Management Science and Engineering at Stanford, is an expert in the field of risk management. She explains that when analyzing a risky situation, it's important to define the possible outcomes and attempt to figure out the chances of each one. Once this is done, one needs to develop a full plan for each eventuality. Elisabeth says it makes sense to take the high risk/high reward path if you're willing to live with all the potential consequences. You should fully prepare for the downside and have a backup plan in place. I encourage you to read the last few sentences several times. Experts in risk management believe you should make decisions based upon the probability of all outcomes, including the best- and worst-case scenarios, and be willing to take big risks when you are fully prepared for all eventualities.

It's also important to remember that good decisions, based on an accurate analysis of the risks involved, can still lead to bad outcomes. That's because risk is still involved. Here is a simple example: soon after I got out of school I was offered a job I wasn't sure was a great fit for me. After several days carefully considering the opportunity, I decided to turn it down, assuming that soon thereafter I would be able to find another job that was a better match. Unfortunately, the economy turned south quite quickly and I spent months looking for another job. I kicked myself for not taking that position, which started to look more and more appealing. I had made a good decision, based upon all the information I had at the time, but in the short run it wasn't a great outcome.

As in this situation, under most circumstances you have to make decisions with incomplete information. That is, you have to make a choice and take action in the face of considerable uncertainty surrounding each option. So, how do you fill in the gaps of your knowledge? I suggest looking to "Stanley" for inspiration. The inner workings of Stanley, the autonomous vehicle designed and built by Stanford's Artificial Intelligence Lab and Volkswagen Electronics Research Laboratory for the DARPA Grand Challenge, offer clues to decision making with incomplete information. DARPA, the Defense Advanced Research Projects Agency, is a government agency charged with the development of cutting-edge technology for the military. In the DARPA competition, driverless cars must navigate a 212-kilometer off-road race. Each must pass through three narrow tunnels, make more than a hundred sharp turns, and navigate mountain passes with steep cliffs on each side. Despite very low odds, Stanford's car won the race, due in large part to its ability to make quick decisions with incomplete information.

Stanley had a lot of powerful technology on board, including three-dimensional maps of the terrain, GPS, gyroscopes, accelerometers, video cameras, and sensors on the wheels. The on-board software analyzed and interpreted all incoming data and controlled the vehicle's speed and direction. But the key to Stanley's victory was its superior skill at making decisions with incomplete information. The designers accomplished this by building in the ability to learn the way humans do. They created a database of human decisions that the car drew upon when making judgments about what to do. This data was incorporated into a learning program tied to the car's control systems, and greatly reduced errors in judgment.

This story highlights the fact that learning from others can significantly reduce your failure rate. You don't have to figure everything out yourself. Like Stanley, you should gather all the data you can from your environment, and then tap into the wisdom of those who have gone before you, in order to make the best possible choice. All you need to do is look around to see hundreds, if not thousands, of role models for every choice you plan to make.

If you do take a risk and happen to fail, remember that you personally are not a failure. The failure is external. This perspective will allow you to get up and try again and again. Your idea might have been poor, the timing might have been off, or you might not have had the necessary resources to succeed. As Jeff Hawkins says, "You are not your company. You are not your product. It is real easy to think you are and it is real easy to get wrapped up in it. . . . But if you fail, or even if you are successful, it is not you. Your company may fail, your product may fail, but you aren't the failure." Keep in mind that failure is a natural part of the learning process. If you aren't failing sometimes, then you probably aren't taking enough risks.

Chapter 6

NO WAY . . . ENGINEERING IS FOR GIRLS

How many people have told you that the key to success is to follow your passions? I'd bet it's a lot. Giving that advice to someone who's struggling to figure out what to do with his or her life is easy. However, that advice is actually simplistic and misleading. Don't get me wrong, I'm a huge fan of passions and think it's incredibly important to know what drives you. But it certainly isn't enough.

Passions are just a starting point. You also need to know your talents and how the world values them. If you're passionate about something but not particularly good at it, then it's going to be pretty frustrating to try to craft a career in that area. Say you love basketball but aren't tall enough to compete, or you're enthralled by jazz but can't carry a tune. In both cases you can be a terrific *fan*, going to games and concerts, without being a professional.

Taking this a step further, perhaps you're passionate about something and are quite talented in the field, but there's no market for those skills. For example, you might be a skilled artist and love to paint, or crave surfing and can ride any wave. But we all know that the market for these skills is small. Trying to craft a career around such passions is often a recipe for frustration. Think of them instead as wonderful *hobbies.*[1]

Alternatively, if you have talent in an area and there's a big market for your skills, then that is a great area to find a *job.* For example, if you are an accomplished accountant, there's always a position for someone who can build a balance sheet. For most people in the world, this is where they live. They have a job that uses their skills, but they can't wait to get home to focus on the activities they love—their hobbies. They count the days until the weekend, until vacation, or until retirement.

The worst-case scenario is finding yourself in a position where you have no passion for your work, no skills in the field, and there's no market for what you're doing. Take the classic joke about trying to sell snow to Eskimos. Now imagine doing that if you hate snow and are a terrible salesperson. This is a bad situation all the way around.

The sweet spot is where your passions overlap with your skills and the market. If you can find that spot, then you're in the wonderful position in which your job enriches your life instead of just providing the financial resources that allow you to enjoy your life *after* the workday is over. The goal should be a *career* in which you can't believe people actually pay you to do your job. A quote attributed to the Chinese Taoist philosopher Lao-Tzu sums this up:

> The master of the art of living makes little distinction between his work and his play, his labor and his leisure, his mind and his body, his education and his recreation, his love and his religion. He simply pursues his vision of excellence in whatever he does, leaving others to decide whether he is working or playing. To him, he is always doing both.

The wisdom of this is reflected in the observation that hard work plays a huge part in making you successful. And, the truth is, we simply tend to work harder at things we're passionate about. This is easy to see in children who spend endless hours working at the things they love to do. A child passionate about building will spend hours designing amazing cities with Legos®. A child who loves art will draw for hours without a break. And to a child who loves sports, shooting hoops or hitting baseballs all afternoon will seem like fun, not practice. Passion is a big driver. It makes each of us want to work hard to perfect our skills and to excel.

The process of finding the gold mine where your skills, interests, and the market collide can take some time. Consider Nathan Furr, who started his academic career as an English major. Nathan was passionate about reading and writing, and spent his college days soaking up turn-of-the-century literature and writing essays that analyzed the work. But he soon realized that the market for English professors was impossibly limited. And even if he got a job in the field, the compensation would be pretty low. This was going to be a tough way to support the big family he was planning. Nathan spent some time thinking about other ways he could use his skills and channel his passions. After scanning the horizon for other options, it became pretty clear that he would fit well in the world of management consulting, which would allow him to use his research and writing skills as well as his joy of learning. The only problem was that Nathan didn't know enough to get that first job in the field. So he gave himself a year to prepare. He joined organizations on his college campus that would allow him to learn more about consulting, and he practiced doing mini–case studies such as those presented during the typical job interview. By the time the one-year mark rolled around, Nathan was ready and landed a prime job as a management consultant for a top firm. It was a great fit in so many ways, tapping into his skills and his passions, and providing him with the financial security he needed.

Nathan picked a career path after he'd been exposed to a variety of options. But most of us are encouraged to plan much further ahead. People love to ask kids, "What do you want to be when you grow up?" This forces children to nail down their goals, at least in their minds, long before they've been exposed to the wide array of opportunities. We also typically visualize ourselves doing the things we see others doing in our immediate environment, which is a terribly limited view considering the world of possibilities. Also, my guess is that you, like me, were heavily influenced by people around you who liked to tell you what *they* thought you should be doing. I clearly remember one of my teachers saying, "You're really good at science. You should consider being a nurse." A fine suggestion, but it is only one of an almost infinite number of things one can do with a gift for science.

During my creativity course, teams of students each pick an organization they think is innovative. These teams visit the firm, interview employees, watch them in action, and come to their own conclusions about what makes the organization creative. They then present this information to the class in an innovative way. One team picked the San Jose Children's Discovery Museum. They followed the staff and visitors for days to see what really made it tick. At one station kids were building a miniature roller coaster, changing different variables to see the results, and an eight-year-old girl was experimenting with the equipment. She changed the length, the height, and the angles of the various parts and ran different simulations to see the effect. A member of the museum staff watched her experimentation for a while and simply commented, "You're doing the same types of things that engineers do." Later that day my students asked the girl what she had learned at the museum. She thought for a second and said with confidence, "I learned that I could be an engineer."

Like the girl in the museum, we all receive explicit and implicit messages about the roles we're expected to play. A couple of years ago a colleague of mine, a mechanical engineering professor, told a remarkable story. She has several women friends from her university who are also engineers in different disciplines. They often came over to her house for dinner and socializing. Her young son was usually around, watching and listening to their conversations. As he got older and proved to be good at math and science someone said to him, "Gee, you should consider studying engineering." He twisted his face and said, "Absolutely not, engineering is for girls." My women friends who are physicians have told me similar stories. Their young sons called discussions about medicine "girl talk."

Consider the following riddle: A boy and his father are in an accident and end up in the hospital. The surgeon says, "I can't operate on this boy, he's my son." What's going on? When I told my very progressive women doctor friends this riddle, even they couldn't figure out that the surgeon in the riddle was the boy's mother. They tried to come up with convoluted answers to the riddle, all involving a male doctor. Once they were told the answer they were terribly embarrassed that they, too, had fallen into this traditional trap.

When I think back on the messages I received, it's clear that specific individuals had a big impact—some were encouraging and others were not. When I was about fourteen years old we had a family friend who was a neurosurgeon. I was fascinated by the brain and finally mustered the courage to ask him about his work. He thought it was "cute" and made a joke. I was disappointed and didn't ask again.

It wasn't until college that I found a professional in the field who explicitly encouraged me to pursue my interest in the brain. I was in my first neuroscience class during my sophomore year and the professor gave us an unusual assignment. He asked us to design a series of experiments to figure out what a specific part of the brain does. He told us that nobody knew its role and that it was our job to come up with a strategy to find out. When I got my paper back a week or so later a note written on the top said, "Tina, you think like a scientist." At that moment I became a scientist. I was just waiting for someone to acknowledge my enthusiasm—and to give me permission to pursue my interests. We are all powerfully influenced by the messages around us. Some are direct, such as a teacher saying, "You should be a nurse," or "You think like a scientist." Others are embedded into our environment, such as years of seeing only female engineers or male surgeons.

When I was in my early twenties, it was surprisingly difficult for me to separate what I wanted for myself and what others wanted for me. I know this is true for many of my students as well. They tell me they're getting so much "guidance" from others that they have a tough time figuring out what they want to do. I remember clearly that I sometimes had the urge to quit or to avoid things that others strongly encouraged me to do, just so I would have the space to figure out what I wanted, independent of what they wanted for me. For example, I started graduate school at the University of Virginia right after I graduated from the University of Rochester. My parents were thrilled. They were so proud of me and were comforted that my path for the next few years was set. But after only one semester of graduate school I decided to take a break and go to California. The hardest part of the entire process was telling my parents I was taking a leave of absence. My decision was extremely hard for them. I appreciated their support and encouragement, but it made it difficult for me to truly know if being in school was the right decision for me. I drove across the country to Santa Cruz with no idea of what I was going to do next.

In retrospect, taking a break from school turned out to be a great choice. My time in Santa Cruz was completely unstructured. I felt like a leaf in the wind, ready for any eventuality. It was exciting and scary. It was the first time I didn't have a specific assignment, a focused goal, or a clear plan. Although often stressful, it was the perfect way to figure out what I really wanted to do. I took odd jobs so I could support myself and spent a lot of time thinking at the beach. After a while I started going to the University of California at Santa Cruz's biology library to keep up on neuroscience literature. At first it was monthly, then weekly, then daily.

After about nine months in Santa Cruz, I was ready to get back into the lab, but not ready to go back to graduate school. With that objective, I tracked down a list of the neuroscience faculty at Stanford University, which was not far away, and wrote each one a letter. I told them about my background and asked if they had a research job for me. Over the next few weeks, I got letters back from all of them, but no one had an open position. However, one faculty member passed my letter on, and I received a call from a professor in the anesthesia department. He asked if I would like to work in the operating room testing new medical equipment on high-risk patients. This seemed interesting, so I jumped at the chance.

Within days I was at Stanford, getting up at the crack of dawn, wearing scrubs, and monitoring surgical patients. This experience was fascinating in a million unexpected ways. Once the project was over, I managed to negotiate a job as a research assistant in a neuroscience lab and eventually applied to graduate school at Stanford. I took detours that might look to others like a waste of time. But this wasn't the case at all. Not only did the twists in my path give me a fresh perspective on my goals, they also gave me time to experiment with options that helped confirm what I wanted to do. Also, this time I was going to graduate school for myself, not for others.

People who are close to you often expect you to make decisions about your career path and stick with them. They want you to be a "fire and forget" missile that zeros in on a target and pursues it relentlessly. But this just isn't how things work. Most people change course many times before finding the best match for their skills and interests. This is similar to the process of developing a product or designing new software—it's important to keep experimenting, trying lots of things until you find out what works. Being too set on your path too early will likely lead you in the wrong direction.

I've met many students who literally show me a detailed map of what they plan to do for the next fifty years. Not only is this unrealistic, but it's sadly limiting. There are so many unexpected experiences ahead that it's best to keep your eyes open instead of blinding yourself to the serendipitous options that might present themselves. Planning a career should be like traveling in a foreign country. Even if you prepare carefully, have an itinerary and a place to stay at night, the most interesting experiences usually aren't planned. You might end up meeting a fascinating person who shows you places that aren't in the guidebook, or you might miss your train and end up spending the day exploring a small town you hadn't planned to visit. I guarantee that the things you're likely to remember from the journey are those that weren't on your original schedule. They will be the unexpected things that jumped in your path, surprising you along the way.

This is true in all endeavors. For example, most major discoveries in science come from paying attention to surprising results and interpreting unexpected findings. Successful scientists quickly learn *not* to be afraid of data that leads them into uncharted territory. Instead of throwing away data that doesn't fit the expected results, writing them off as artifacts, the best scientists latch on to anomalies, knowing this is where true breakthroughs are made. In fact, by being alert to inconsistencies, scientists often open entirely new fields of research and make remarkable discoveries. For example, from the early days of microscopy, in the mid-1800s, scientists saw that there were two general classes of cells in the brain, which they called neurons and glia. They assumed that all the real action happened in the neurons and that the glia, which literally means glue in Greek, served only as a kind of "scaffolding," or structural support for neurons. This idea held for over 150 years, and scientists spent most their efforts studying neurons.

However, over the past twenty years, glia, which are more abundant in the brain than neurons by a factor of ten, have been found to serve an enormous number of important roles in the nervous system. Bruce Ransom, the founding editor of the scientific journal *Glia,* is a pioneer in this field. He and other scientists around the world have demonstrated that glial cells are active participants in virtually every function of the brain. Even synaptic transmission, the most studied interaction between neurons, involves glial cells. Bruce, who is also a neurologist, believes that glia have not yet given up all their secrets and are critically involved in many neurological diseases.

This is an important reminder that ideas can be so attractive that they actually impede progress. People latch onto them and don't see the other viable alternatives; they unconsciously "adjust" conflicting observations to fit prevailing theories. In retrospect, it seems obvious that glia serve an important role in the brain. But those who began doing research in this area two decades ago were taking a risk by stepping off a clearly defined path to explore uncharted territory.

Most events and findings snap into focus when looked at in retrospect. Randy Komisar claims that his career makes much more sense when viewed through the rearview mirror than through the windshield. This statement is true for most of us. When you look back on your career path the story makes perfect sense. The road ahead, however, is always fuzzy and full of boundless uncertainty. It's easy to get frustrated by the lack of visibility ahead. You can, however, do things to increase the odds that great opportunities will come your way.

Randy has spent considerable time thinking about how to craft a career, and his insights are powerful. He suggests that you build a career in such a way that you optimize the quality of the people with whom you work, which ends up increasing the quality of the opportunities that flow your way. Great people support each other, build valuable networks, and create a steady stream of new opportunities. Essentially, the ecosystem in which you live and work is a huge factor in predicting the types of opportunities that will present themselves.

Many seasoned professionals echo his ideas. They know it's a mistake to try to manage your career too closely, and that you should instead work in organizations that grant you access to a stream of interesting opportunities. Teresa Briggs, the managing partner of the Silicon Valley office of Deloitte, a large international professional services firm, gave up the notion that she could plan everything in favor of being much more opportunistic. Teresa began her career in the audit practice of Deloitte and after eighteen years reasonably assumed she would be there forever. However, she eventually found herself in an unpredictable situation. New laws required auditors to rotate on and off assignments with individual clients so a fresh set of auditors could ensure the business was being managed legally. Teresa had been working with a very large client, and when she rotated off the team there weren't other comparable opportunities. But she learned that a new Deloitte group was forming that focused on mergers and acquisitions. While mergers and acquisitions was not her area of expertise, she was offered the opportunity to take a key position. She found that her skills transferred beautifully. Even though Teresa would not have planned this path herself, she realized that her ability to build relationships with clients and lead teams allowed her to excel in this new role.

After a short time, Teresa was transferred to the Deloitte national office in New York, where her leadership and management skills again allowed her to shine. Teresa was then asked to head up the Silicon Valley practice for the firm, where she had to learn new strategies and a brand-new vocabulary, this time for high technology. None of Teresa's steps could have been predicted, and yet, by excelling in an organization that presented a continuous flow of new opportunities, many exciting roles and challenges materialized.

• • •

It is important to reassess your life and career relatively frequently. This self-assessment process forces you to come to terms with the fact that sometimes it's time to move on to a new environment in order to excel. Most people don't assess their roles frequently enough and so stay in positions for years longer than they should, settling for suboptimal situations. There isn't a magic number for the amount of time you should stay in one role before evaluating whether it's right or not. But it makes sense to think about how often you do so. Some people readjust their lives daily or weekly, constantly optimizing. Others wait years before noticing that they've ended up far from where they had hoped to be. The more frequently you assess your situation, looking for ways to fix problems, the more likely you are to find yourself in a position where things are going well. It's best to address small problems that crop up in your life early and often, as opposed to waiting for problems to get so big that they seem intractable. That can only happen when you pay attention and figure out what actually needs to change.

Some situations literally force you to reevaluate your life. For instance, once you decide to start a family, the entire game changes. You're suddenly faced with the need to figure out how to balance parenting with your profession. As everyone knows, caring for young children takes an enormous amount of time and focused energy. It's both physically and emotionally demanding, and incredibly time consuming. Keeping you on your toes, a child's needs change dramatically as they get older. Each year brings a brand-new set of responsibilities and a fresh set of challenges. As a result, parenting provides an ever-changing opportunity to be creative and helps build skills that are extremely valuable in any setting. It exercises your ability to multitask and to make decisions under pressure, and it certainly helps you master the art of negotiation.

Women especially face the daunting puzzle of figuring out how to fit together career and family obligations. From my experience, this challenge really is a great opportunity. Instead of considering traditional jobs that have limited flexibility, being a parent forces you to be innovative. Additionally, as your child's needs change, you can experiment with different jobs with different responsibilities. Although it is hard to see up close, one's career is long, and children are small for only a few years, allowing you to accelerate your career as your children grow up. The following excerpt from a 1997 edition of *Stanford Magazine* puts a sharp point on this idea.

> A 1950 [Stanford] graduate earned her law degree here in '52, and took five years out of the paid workforce after her second son was born, keeping herself busy and visible in volunteer work for the Phoenix Junior League and the Salvation Army. Later, when her youngest went off to school, she went back to work part-time in the state attorney general's office.
>
> Staying home with her children during those years ultimately didn't hamper her career. . . . She added that

today's young graduates could fare even better than she did. "One help is that nowadays women live longer," she says. "We spend more years in employment and really have time for a couple of careers. So if a few years are taken out, all is not lost."

The woman, by the way, is Supreme Court Justice Sandra Day O'Connor.

From my experience, this is absolutely right. My only recommendation is that if you intend to stop working while your kids are young, consider finding a way to keep your career on a low simmer. If you haven't stepped all the way out for too long, it's much easier to get back in. You can do this in an infinite variety of ways, from working part-time in traditional jobs to volunteering. Not only does it keep your skills sharpened, but it provides you with the confidence that you can gear up again when you're ready.

Consider Karen Matthys, who has four young children and is part of a group of part-time marketing consultants. Karen takes on projects when she can, and hands them over to her partners when she's too busy. Or take Lisa Benatar, who with young three daughters turned her attention to her children's school. Lisa, an expert on alternative energy, started an educational program at the school that focused on teaching children about conservation.

Taking on the puzzle of balancing work and parenting ended up being the best career decision I ever made. I wanted to be intellectually stimulated without compromising the time I had for my son. As a result, each year I evaluated how much time I needed to devote to each and found ways to take on projects that allowed me the most flexibility. I took on assignments I probably wouldn't have considered if I didn't have a child. I started writing children's books, launched a Web site for science teachers, and even taught science in a private elementary school. In the long run, these experiences proved to be amazingly helpful when I did go back to work full-time. I gained credibility as a writer, learned how to design Web sites, and got valuable experience teaching—all skills I use every single day in my current role.

Looking back, I see many things I wish I had known about crafting a career that were counter to the traditional advice I was given. Most important? The need to find a role in the world that doesn't feel like work. This only happens when you identify the intersection between your skills, your passions, and the market. Not only is this the most fulfilling position, but, by tapping into your passions in a constructive way, your work enriches your life, as opposed to taking time away from it. Finding the right roles requires experimenting along the way, trying lots of different alternatives, testing the messages you get both explicitly and implicitly from the world, and pushing back on those that just don't feel right.

As you move through your career, you will be well served by frequently reassessing where you are and where you want to go. Doing so allows you to make course corrections quickly, especially when things don't turn out as planned or exceptional new opportunities arise. Don't worry that the path ahead appears out of focus—squinting isn't going to make it any clearer. This is true for everyone. Don't be in a rush to get to your final destination—the side trips and unexpected detours quite often lead to the most interesting people, places, and opportunities. And, finally, be wary of all career advice, including mine, as you figure out what's right for you.

Chapter 7

TURN LEMONADE INTO HELICOPTERS

I called my son, Josh, during his first semester at college to wish him luck on his final exams. His response was, "There's no such thing as luck. It's all hard work." He's a driven kid, who throws himself at the things about which he is passionate, especially athletic competitions that require a tremendous amount of training and preparation. At first I thought his response was extreme. But, on further reflection, I believe he had it right. Even when we think we're lucky, we've usually worked remarkably hard to put ourselves in that position.

I've watched Josh with admiration as he has strived to meet goals others might think impossible. At nineteen, he decided to try his hand at competitive powerlifting. This wasn't a natural choice for a former cyclist and track sprinter, but he was determined to break the national record for dead lifts. Josh identified the best trainers in northern California and drove two hours each way, several times a week, to learn from them. He read everything he could about the sport, carefully crafted a diet to build more muscle, and spent hours training at the gym. After several years of weight training followed by months of focused effort, he entered a competition to see how he stacked up against others. We arose at 5:00 a.m. and drove three hours to Fresno for a formal meet. The gym was filled with weight lifters who'd been competing for years. I was worried he would be disappointed with his performance. But Josh, weighing in at 190 pounds, blew away both the federation's state and national records by lifting 589.7 pounds—this was 50 pounds more than the previous record holder. Was he lucky? Of course he was lucky. All the cards aligned for him that day. But he would never have succeeded unless he had put tremendous effort behind his goals.

Josh's comments on luck echoed the message I frequently heard from my father when I was a child—the harder you work, the luckier you get. His mantra was a stark reminder that you need to put yourself in a position to be lucky. Even if there's a low probability of success and a tremendous amount of competition, you can maximize your chances by being well prepared physically, intellectually, and emotionally.

We often hear inspiring stories about people who start with nothing and by virtue of incredibly hard work are able to draw luck their way. Here are two quick stories that probably sound familiar, of people who worked incredibly hard to overcome tremendous hardships.

Quyen Vuong was born in Saigon, Vietnam, where her father worked for the Vietnamese government and her mother ran a pharmacy. As the daughter of professionals, her young life was very comfortable. However, when the Communists overran the country in 1975, Quyen's world was turned upside down. Her father was sent to a reeducation camp, her family's pharmacy was shuttered, and her mother was sent to prison for being a "capitalist" because she ran her own business. Within a few years it was clear their situation wasn't improving, and her father left for the United States with two of Quyen's siblings. The rest of the family stayed behind in Vietnam.

The following year, 1980, Quyen's mother felt compelled to send Quyen, age sixteen, and her younger brother, age eleven, in search of a better life. She tearfully put them on a boat with other refugees, hoping they would ultimately make it to the United States. She had little confidence that they would complete the journey or that she would ever see her children again. Following many days at sea, dodging pirates who tried to steal the few belongings brought by the refugees, the boat finally landed on an island off the coast of Malaysia. There the boat's passengers joined more than forty thousand refugees, each struggling to survive and trying desperately to obtain permission to immigrate to another country.

After four long months, Quyen was permitted to join her father in Texas. She spoke no English and was subsequently held back in school by several years. Her family was so poor that she and her siblings each worked at least thirty hours a week after school. Quyen often thought about dropping out to better support her family, which was surviving on a week-to-week basis, often forced to call upon relatives for loans.

Despite the hardships, Quyen worked as steadfastly as she could. She had nothing but her self-motivation to pull herself out of poverty. She finished high school near the top of her class and went on to Yale with a full scholarship. After studying economics and then earning an MBA, Quyen now runs ICAN, a not-for-profit company that serves the Vietnamese community by helping immigrants bridge cultural gaps, so they can thrive in their new country. She now provides the services she wishes she had available when she made it to her new homeland.

As a young girl, Quyen had no idea what she wanted to accomplish as an adult, but she did know with certainty that she wanted to pull herself out of poverty. She feels that by setting the table with time and effort you ensure that something appealing will land on your plate. Quyen's experience has taught her that, as she says, "You can make your own destiny by focusing on your goals and working incredibly hard."

I heard a similar story from Quincy Delight Jones III, aka QD3, a successful music and film producer who has worked with well-known artists such as Tupac Shakur, LL Cool J, and Ice Cube.[1] As the son of the music legend Quincy Jones, you might think QD3 had an easy life. He didn't. His parents divorced when he was young and his mother brought him to Sweden, her native country, where they lived in near poverty.

His mother had an alternative lifestyle and struggled with drug addiction. She didn't particularly care if QD3 went to school, and she often didn't come home from partying until 4:00 in the morning.

From the time QD3 was exposed to break dancing in his early teens he was hooked. He started performing on the streets in Stockholm, putting out a hat to collect donations from passersby. He practiced his dance moves day and night, perfecting each one. With "luck" he was discovered by a scout from Levi's, who asked if he would be interested in going on a performance tour. QD3 jumped at the chance.

Once he had his foot in the door, QD3 continued to work as hard as he could. Besides dancing, he started developing music beats for rap artists. A big break came when he was asked to write the sound track for a movie about the rap scene in Stockholm. One of his songs, "Next Time," written when he was sixteen, became his first gold record and sold over fifty thousand copies. QD3 went on to produce a triple platinum documentary about Tupac Shakur, which sold more than three hundred thousand copies.

Just like Quyen, QD3 was driven to pull himself out of poverty, to be self-sufficient and, ultimately, the best in the world. He "taps the fire in his heart" to motivate himself, and once the flame spreads, charges ahead with incredible commitment and effort. Both Quyen and QD3 throw everything they have—physically, intellectually, and emotionally—at the problems confronting them, demonstrating that hard work and dedication are key to tempting luck your way. However, hard work is just one lever at your disposal when it comes to making your own luck. There are many other tools in your toolbox that can serve as luck magnets. And I'm confident that both Quyen and QD3 used these, as well.

Richard Wiseman, of the University of Hertfordshire in England, has studied luck and found that "lucky people" share traits that tend to make them luckier than others. First, lucky people take advantage of chance occurrences that come their way. Instead of going through life on cruise control, they pay attention to what's happening around them and, therefore, are able to extract greater value from each situation. They're more likely to pay attention to an announcement for a special event in their community, to notice a new person in their neighborhood, or even to see that a colleague is in need of some extra help. Lucky people are also open to novel opportunities and willing to try things outside of their usual experiences. They're more inclined to pick up a book on an unfamiliar subject, to travel to less familiar destinations, and to interact with people who are different than themselves.

Not surprisingly, lucky people tend to be extraverted. They make more eye contact and smile more frequently, leading to more positive and extended encounters. These actions, in turn, open the door to more opportunities. Lucky people also tend to be optimistic and to expect good things to happen to them. This becomes a self-fulfilling prophecy, because even when things don't go as expected, lucky people find ways to extract positive outcomes from the worst situations. Their attitude affects those around them, and helps to turn negative situations into positive experiences.

In short, being observant, open-minded, friendly, and optimistic invites luck your way. Take this simple story: several years ago I was at a small local grocery store frequented mostly by those who live nearby. A man and his young daughter approached me in the frozen-food aisle and politely asked how to prepare frozen, canned lemonade. The man had an accent I couldn't identify, and I was pretty sure he must be new to the area. I told him how to prepare the lemonade and asked where he was from. He said Santiago, Chile. I asked his name and what brought him to our town. I had no ulterior motive. I was just curious. He told me his name was Eduardo and that he and his family were in the area for a year so he could learn about entrepreneurship in Silicon Valley. He was in line to run his family's business and was in search of tools to make it more innovative. I told him about the entrepreneurship program at Stanford's School of Engineering and said I'd be happy to do what I could to be of help. Over the next few months I introduced Eduardo to various people in the entrepreneurship community, and he expressed his thanks for my assistance.

Fast-forward two years. I was heading for a conference in Santiago and sent Eduardo a message asking if he wanted to get together for coffee. At the last minute, he wasn't able to make it, but invited me to go to a specific location in downtown Santiago with a few of my colleagues. We showed up at the office building and were led to the roof, where we were picked up by Eduardo's family's private helicopter for a simply spectacular ride above the city, up to the surrounding mountains, and over his family's ski resort. It was incredible! And to think that it resulted from helping him figure out how to make lemonade. Of course, I didn't help Eduardo because I wanted a helicopter ride. But by putting myself out there, being open to helping someone, and following up years later, I became quite "lucky." Earlier I discuss the art of turning lemons (problems) into lemonade (opportunities). But luck goes beyond this—it's about turning lemonade (good things) into helicopters (amazing things!).

The world is full of doors through which we can find a staggering array of opportunities—we just have to be willing to open them. Carlos Vignolo, from the University of Chile, likes to say that if you go somewhere and don't meet someone new, you have certainly missed out on making a friend as well as on the possibility of making a million dollars. He tells his students that every time they walk onto a city bus, a million dollars is waiting there for them—they just have to find it. In this case "a million dollars" is a metaphor for learning something new, making a friend, or, indeed, making a million dollars. In fact, this book is the direct result of my talking with someone sitting next to me on an airplane. If we hadn't started a conversation,

I most certainly wouldn't have written this book. But that's another story.

Echoing this point, Tom Kelley, author of *The Art of Innovation*, says that every day you should act like a foreign traveler by being acutely aware of your environment. In everyday life we tend to put on blinders and cruise down well-worn paths, rarely stopping to look around. But as a traveler in a foreign country, you see the world with fresh eyes and dramatically increase the density of your experiences. By tuning in, you find fascinating things around every turn.

James Barlow, the head of the Scottish Institute for Enterprise, does a provocative exercise with his students to demonstrate this point. He gives jigsaw puzzles to several teams and sets a timer to see which group can finish first. The puzzle pieces have been numbered on the back, from 1 to 500, so it's easy to put them together if you just pay attention to the numbers. But, even though the numbers are right in front of them, it takes most teams a long time to see them, and some never see them at all. Essentially, they could easily bolster their luck just by paying closer attention.

Paying careful attention to your environment actually takes a lot of effort. You have to teach yourself to do it well, and even when you're paying attention, you can miss really interesting and important information that's right in front of you. A widely distributed video shows this all too clearly. An audience is asked to watch a group of men and women tossing around a basketball. They're told to count the number of times the team in white shirts passes the ball. At the end of the video, viewers can easily answer that question, but are oblivious to the fact that someone in a bear suit moonwalks right through the game.[2] Even when we think we're paying full attention, there's usually so much more to see.

I do a simple exercise in my class that illustrates this clearly. I send students to a familiar location, such as the local shopping center, and ask them to complete a "lab" in which they go to several stores and pay attention to all the things that are normally "invisible." They take the time to notice the sounds, smells, textures, and colors, as well as the organization of the merchandise and the way the staff interacts with the customers. They observe endless things they never saw when they previously zipped in and out of the same environment. They come back with their eyes wide open, realizing that we all tend to walk through life with blinders on.

Lucky people don't just pay attention to the world around them and meet interesting individuals—they also find unusual ways to use and recombine their knowledge and experiences. Most people have remarkable resources at their fingertips, but never figure out how to leverage them. However, lucky people appreciate the value of their knowledge and their network, and tap into these gold mines as needed. Here's a powerful example from the 2005 commencement address that Steve Jobs delivered at Stanford. In short, he'd dropped out of college after six months because he wasn't sure why he was there, and the tuition was much more than his parents could afford. Here's how Steve tells it:

> After six months, I couldn't see the value in [college]. I had no idea what I wanted to do with my life and no idea how college was going to help me figure it out. And here I was spending all of the money my parents had saved their entire life. So I decided to drop out and trust that it would all work out OK. It was pretty scary at the time, but looking back it was one of the best decisions I ever made. The minute I dropped out I could stop taking the required classes that didn't interest me, and begin dropping in on the ones that looked interesting.
>
> It wasn't all romantic. I didn't have a dorm room, so I slept on the floor in friends' rooms, I returned Coke bottles for the five cent deposits to buy food with, and I would walk the seven miles across town every Sunday night to get one good meal a week at the Hare Krishna temple. I loved it. And much of what I stumbled into by following my curiosity and intuition turned out to be priceless later on. Let me give you one example:
>
> Reed College at that time offered perhaps the best calligraphy instruction in the country. Throughout the campus every poster, every label on every drawer, was beautifully hand calligraphed. Because I had dropped out and didn't have to take the normal classes, I decided to take a calligraphy class to learn how to do this. I

> learned about serif and san serif typefaces, about varying the amount of space between different letter combinations, about what makes great typography great. It was beautiful, historical, artistically subtle in a way that science can't capture, and I found it fascinating.
>
> None of this had even a hope of any practical application in my life. But ten years later, when we were designing the first Macintosh computer, it all came back to me. And we designed it all into the Mac. It was the first computer with beautiful typography. If I had never dropped in on that single course in college, the Mac would have never had multiple typefaces or proportionally spaced fonts. And since Windows just copied the Mac, it's likely that no personal computer would have them. If I had never dropped out, I would have never dropped in on this calligraphy class, and personal computers might not have the wonderful typography that they do. Of course it was impossible to connect the dots looking forward when I was in college. But it was very, very clear looking backwards ten years later.

This story emphasizes that you never know when your experiences will prove to be valuable. Steve Jobs was open-minded and curious about the world, collected diverse experiences independent of their short-term benefits, and was able to tap into his knowledge in unexpected ways. This is a sharp reminder that the more experiences you have and the broader your base of knowledge, the more resources you have from which to draw.

In my course on creativity I focus a great deal on the value of recombining ideas in unusual ways. The more you practice this skill, the more natural it becomes. For example, using similes or metaphors, to describe concepts that on the surface seem completely unrelated offers tools for revealing fresh solutions to familiar problems. We do a simple exercise to illustrate this point. Teams are asked to come up with as many answers as possible to the following statement:

Ideas are like ____________________________________
because ____,
therefore ______________________________________.

Below is a list of some of the hundreds of creative answers I've seen. In each case the simile unlocks a new way of looking at ideas:

- Ideas are like babies because everyone thinks theirs is cute, therefore be objective when judging your own ideas.
- Ideas are like shoes because you need to break them in, therefore take time to evaluate new ideas.
- Ideas are like mirrors because they reflect the local environment, therefore consider changing contexts to get more diverse collections of ideas.

- Ideas are like hiccups because when they start they don't stop, therefore take advantage of idea streaks.
- Ideas are like bubbles because they easily burst, therefore be gentle with them.
- Ideas are like cars because they take you places, therefore go along for the ride.
- Ideas are like chocolates because everyone loves them, therefore make sure to serve them up frequently.
- Ideas are like the measles because they are contagious, therefore hang out with other people with ideas if you want to get them yourself.
- Ideas are like waffles because they are best when fresh, therefore keep new ideas coming all the time.
- Ideas are like spider webs because they are stronger than they appear, therefore don't underestimate them.

This exercise encourages you to stretch your imagination by tapping into the world around you for inspiration. Some people make these connections naturally and find unusual ways to extract value from them. Like Steve Jobs, those people are always scouting for ways to bring ideas together in interesting ways and then make the effort to bring their ideas to life.

A great example is Perry Klebahn, who broke his ankle in 1991. The injury was especially disappointing to this avid skier who didn't want to miss a season on the slopes. However, he found a way to turn his bad fortune into good luck. While recovering from the injury, he discovered an old pair of wooden snowshoes and took them out for a spin, hoping this would provide an alternative to skiing. They didn't work well at all, which was another disappointment. But instead of throwing them back into his closet and waiting for his ankle to heal, Perry decided to design a new snowshoe. He was a product design student at the time and figured he could use these new skills to solve his own problem. Over the course of ten weeks, he designed and built eight different versions of snowshoes. On weekdays he built prototypes in the school machine shop, and over weekends he went to the mountains to try them out. By the end of the tenth week he was ready to file patents on his innovations.

Once the design was perfected, Perry hand-built some snowshoes and set out to sell them to sporting goods stores. The buyers took one look at them and asked, "What are these?" They were unlike anything they had seen before and there was *no* market for snowshoes. But Perry persevered, knowing there must be lots of people who couldn't ski for one reason or another but still wanted a way to spend time in the mountains during the winter. In the end, he decided to build the market himself.

Perry personally took sporting goods salespeople to the snow-covered mountains each weekend to let them try out his invention. He told them there was no obligation to promote snowshoes to their customers; he just wanted them to get a taste of this new sport. The salespeople loved the experience and passed the news on to the buyers at their stores. As a result, sporting goods stores started stocking Perry's new product. But the challenge didn't stop there.

After customers purchased Perry's new snowshoes, they had no clue where to use them. So Perry had to convince ski resorts around the United States to promote snowshoeing. He encouraged them to create special snowshoe trails, to make maps for their customers, to provide trail passes, and to monitor the trails to keep them safe. Once done, the pieces were in place for the snowshoe market to balloon, and it grew from zero dollars to $50 million. Perry's company, Atlas Snowshoe, was subsequently sold to K2, and snowshoes and well-marked trails for snowshoeing are now widely available.

Perry turned a series of bad breaks—literal and figurative—into a winning streak by seeing opportunities and connecting the dots between his broken ankle, his desire to spend time in the snow, his new product design skills, and his astute observation that others would benefit from a better snowshoe. He ultimately made out well, but only after huge investments of time, energy, and perseverance. Many people would have given up along the way, balking or even stopping at each new obstacle. But Perry saw opportunities in every challenge, and as each hurdle was overcome and all the pieces were put in place, his chances of seeing a positive end result increased. This only happened because Perry used every skill described by Richard Wiseman. He was observant, outgoing, adventurous, and optimistic, as well as hard-working. Each of these traits was important in contributing to his ultimate good.

While Perry worked incredibly hard to overcome obstacles in order to create his own luck, there are many examples of individuals making luck by fearlessly looking for exciting opportunities. A compelling example is found in Dana Calderwood's story. Dana loved the theater and spent countless hours involved in school plays, starting when he was in high school. We were classmates at Summit High School in New Jersey, where we were both serious "drama freaks." Acting was a hobby for me, but Dana had dreams of being a director, and started cooking up his own luck in order to optimize the chances of making that happen long before he left high school.

As stated above, Dana was fearless. He had the gumption to ask the head of the drama department if he could direct the next major school play. No student had ever asked for that role before, but the teacher agreed. Dana didn't wait to be anointed by someone in authority; he simply asked for what he wanted. That moment launched Dana's directing career. He went on to direct plays at the local Metropolitan Musical Theater, where a visiting alumni director, who had since gone on to a successful career in Hollywood, gave him some sage advice. He told Dana that the skills he was using at the theater company were the same skills needed in the big leagues. This advice gave Dana the confidence to set his sights even higher.

Dana went on to study at New York University's film school, and while there squeezed the juice out of every opportunity.

Dana always stayed after classes to meet guest speakers, and he asked them for follow-up meetings and names of other people he should contact. He also learned to make the most of every film assignment. At first, like his classmates, he used his friends as actors in his films (this is how I got my film debut in Dana's version of the famous shower scene in *Psycho*). However, Dana soon realized there was an opportunity to invite famous actors to star in his pieces. One TV production class assignment involved creating a short program for television. Most of Dana's classmates conducted simple interviews with one another to satisfy the requirement, but Dana asked the Academy Award–winning actress, Estelle Parsons, who was in the midst of performing in a Tony-nominated play, to participate—and she agreed. Again, he made himself lucky by paying attention to nonobvious but exciting alternatives. He put himself out there by asking for what he wanted.

As time went on, Dana took on bigger and bigger challenges, and eventually, he was asked to be the director for *Late Night with Conan O'Brien*, which he did for years before directing many more shows, including *Rachel Ray* and *The Iron Chef*. Had Dana seen his adult self when he was twenty, he would have been in awe of his good luck. Dana's fortune comes from putting everything he knows into everything he does. He is fearless about asking for opportunities to do things he has never done before, and with each successful leap gains additional insights and knowledge that help him take on the next bigger challenge.

Dana long ago internalized the idea that directing on a small stage is similar to directing on a big stage, and this gave him the confidence to jump to ever-larger stepping-stones as he literally made opportunities present themselves. Many people don't feel comfortable making such leaps, preferring instead to stay in smaller venues. And one could argue that there are many advantages to working with intimate teams on small projects. Others dream of a bigger stage, but are daunted by the perceived distance between where they are and where they want to go. Dana's story shows that by seizing all the opportunities around us, we can slowly but surely pull ourselves from stage to stage, each time drawing ourselves closer to our final objective.

As we have seen, we can manufacture our own luck by working incredibly hard and focusing on our goals. But we have many other tools at our disposal, including being open to opportunities that come our way, taking full advantage of chance occurrences, paying careful attention to the world around us, interacting with as many people as we can, and making those interactions as positive as possible. Making one's own luck is ultimately about turning bad situations around and making good situations much better. We dramatically increase the chances that we will be lucky by exposing ourselves to as many diverse experiences as possible, boldly recombining these experiences in unusual ways, and fearlessly striving to get to the stage on which we want to play out our life.

Chapter 8

PAINT THE TARGET AROUND THE ARROW

Who would have thought that the package of notecards my mother gave me for my tenth birthday would have been one of the most valuable gifts I have ever received. They were light blue and said "Tina" in block letters on the top. At that age my mother taught me how to write a thank-you note and how important they are. She couldn't have been more correct. In fact, as I grew up and ultimately entered the work world, I often tried to channel my mother, who always seemed to know what to do in social settings. But the importance of writing thank-you notes remains one of her most valuable lessons.

Showing appreciation for the things others do for you has a profound effect on how you're perceived. Keep in mind that everything someone does for you has an opportunity cost. That means if someone takes time out of his or her day to attend to you, there's something they haven't done for themselves or for someone else. It's easy to fool yourself into thinking your request is small. But when someone is busy there are no small requests. They have to stop what they're doing, focus on your request, and take the time to respond. With that in mind, there is never a time when you shouldn't thank someone for doing something for you. In fact, assume a thank-you note is in order, and look at situations when you don't send one as the exception. Because so few people actually do this (unfortunately), you will certainly stand out from the crowd.

Some of the other little things that make a big difference in your life are simple, while others are more challenging. Some are intuitive and others surprising. Some are taught in schools but most are not. Over the years I've stumbled many times, sometimes irreversibly, by not understanding these "little things."

First and foremost, remember that there are only fifty people in the world. Of course, this isn't true literally. But it often feels that way because you're likely to bump into people you know, or people who know the people you know, all over the world. The person sitting next to you might become your boss, your employee, your customer, or your sister-in-law. Over the course of your life, the same people will quite likely play many different roles. I've had many occasions where individuals who were once my superiors later came to me for help, and I've found myself going to people who were once my subordinates for guidance. The roles we play continue to change in surprising ways over time, and you will be amazed by the people who keep showing up in your life.

Because we live in such a small world, it really is important not to burn bridges, no matter how tempted you might be. You aren't going to like everyone and everyone isn't going to like you, but there's no need to make enemies. For example, when you look for your next job, it's quite likely that the person interviewing you will know someone you know. In this way your reputation precedes you everywhere you go. This is beneficial when you have a great reputation, but harmful when your reputation is damaged.

I've seen the following scenario play out innumerable times. Imagine you're interviewing for a job that has dozens of candidates. The interview goes well and you appear to be a great match for the position. During the meeting, the interviewer looks at your résumé and realizes that you used to work with an old friend of hers. After the interview, she makes a quick call to her friend to ask about you. A casual comment from her friend about your past performance can seal the deal or cut you off at the knees. In many cases you will believe the job was in the bag, right before you receive a rejection letter. You'll never know what hit you.

Essentially, your reputation is your most valuable asset—so guard it well. But don't be terribly demoralized if you make some mistakes along the way. With time it is possible to repair a stained reputation. Over the years I've come up with a metaphor that has helped me put this in perspective: every experience you have with someone else is like a drop of water falling into a pool. As your experiences with that person grow, the drops accumulate and the pool deepens. Positive interactions are clear drops of water and negative interactions are red drops of water. But they aren't equal. That is, a number of clear drops can dilute one red drop, and that number differs for different people. Those who are very forgiving only need a few positive experiences—clear drops—to dilute a bad experience, while those who are less forgiving need a lot more to wash away the red. Also, for most people the pool drains slowly. As a result, we tend to pay attention to the experiences that have happened most recently, as opposed to those that happened a long time ago. This metaphor implies that if you have a large reserve of positive experiences with someone, then one red drop is hardly noticed. It's like putting a drop of red ink into the ocean. But if you don't know a person well, one bad experience stains the pool bright red. You can wash away negative interactions by flooding the pool with positive interactions until the red drops fade, but the deeper the red, the more work you have to do to cleanse the pool. I've found that sometimes the pool color never clears; when that happens, it's time to stop interacting with that particular person.

This serves as a reminder of the importance of every experience we have with others, whether they are friends, family, co-workers, or service providers. In fact, some organizations actually capture information about how you treat them, and that influences how they treat you. For example, at some well-known business schools, every interaction a candidate has with the school or its personnel is noted. If a candidate is rude to the receptionist, this is recorded in his or her file and comes into play when admissions decisions are made. This also happens at companies such as JetBlue. According to Bob Sutton's *The No Asshole Rule*, if you're consistently rude to JetBlue's staff, you will get blacklisted and find it strangely impossible to get a seat on their planes.

Obviously, you can't make everyone happy all the time, and some of your actions are going to ruffle feathers. One way to figure out how to handle these situations is to imagine how you will describe what happened later, when the dust has cleared. I'm reminded of a case a few years ago when a student came to me for advice. He was leading the campus-wide business plan competition and one team didn't show up for the final round of judging. Like all the teams that reach that stage of the competition, the team had been working on the project for seven months and had managed to make it over a lot of hurdles to get to the finish line. The team hadn't received the message about the presentation time, in part because it was posted late and in part because they weren't paying attention. The student who came to ask my opinion was torn about what to do. He felt there were two clear choices: he could hold fast to the rules and disqualify the team, or he could be flexible and find another time for them to present their work. His gut reaction was to stick to the rules. Everyone else had managed to show up, and it was going to be a burden to reschedule. The only guidance I gave him was this: whatever he did, I hoped he would be pleased with his decision at a later date. I urged him to consider how he would describe this challenge if during a job interview he were asked how he handled an ambiguous situation. The delinquent team was subsequently allowed to present, and I realized afterward that thinking about how you want to tell the story in the future is a great way to assess your response to dilemmas in general. Craft the story now so you'll be proud to tell it later.

Everyone makes mistakes, and floundering is part of life, especially when you're doing things for the first time. I've spent countless hours kicking myself for stupid things I've done. However, I've also figured out that learning how to recover from those mistakes is key. For instance, knowing how to apologize is incredibly important. A simple acknowledgment that you messed up goes a long way. There's no need for long speeches and explanations; just say, "I didn't handle that very well. I apologize." The sooner you do this after recognizing your mistake, the better. If you wait a long time to apologize, the damage continues to grow.

I've had many chances to practice recovering from errors. This story is particularly memorable: soon after I got out of school, I read an article in the local newspaper about plans to build the San Jose Technology Museum. It sounded like an amazing place to work. Jim Adams, a Stanford professor known for his pioneering work on creativity, would be the museum's director. I called the museum office daily in an attempt to reach him, but each time was told Jim wasn't there. Although I didn't leave messages, the receptionist learned to recognize my voice and informed Jim every time I called. By the time I reached him, Jim had a stack of messages from me that was nearly an inch tall.

Jim finally agreed to meet with me. I managed to pass the test with him during the interview, but there really was no formal job to offer me and he ultimately suggested I talk with the woman who had recently been hired to lead the exhibit design effort. It's not unlikely that her first assignment was to get rid of me. She invited me to lunch for an interview, but before we'd even ordered she said, "I just want to tell you that you're not a good match for this organization. You're just too pushy." I felt tears welling up and had to think fast to pull out of the tailspin. I apologized, told her I appreciated the feedback, and said that most people would call me high energy and enthusiastic. I told her it was helpful to know I had inadvertently misrepresented myself. Clearly, my enthusiasm had been misinterpreted. The tension melted, we had a fascinating conversation, and I walked away with a job offer.

This story demonstrates that it is important to take responsibility for your actions and be willing to learn from your experiences. Once that happens, you can quickly move on. And echoing an earlier point, the course I now teach on creativity at Stanford, in the School of Engineering, was first taught by Jim Adams many years ago. It really is a very small world!

I recently learned from Jeannie Kahwajy, an expert on interpersonal interactions, that her research shows that those who demonstrate that they are willing to learn can turn negative situations around very effectively. Jeannie ran experiments involving mock interviews by recruiters of job candidates. The recruiter was primed beforehand to have a negative bias toward the candidate. Of the three groups of candidates, one was instructed to *prove* they should get the job; one was told to *learn* from the interaction; and the final group, the control, was given no specific instructions. She found that the recruiter's negative bias was reinforced for both the control group and the group that tried to prove they should get the job. However, the candidates who set out to learn from the interaction reversed the recruiter's negative bias.

Another essential life skill rarely taught in school is the ability to negotiate. Most of our interactions with others are essentially a series of negotiations, and we do ourselves a huge disservice by not knowing the basic tenets. We negotiate with our friends about what to do on Saturday night, we negotiate with our family about who does the dishes and who pays the bills, we negotiate with our colleagues about who will stay late to complete an assignment, and we negotiate with salespeople on the price of a car. We negotiate all day, but most of us don't even realize it, nor do we have a clue how to do it well.

I run an exercise in class that on the surface appears to be a simple negotiation between a job candidate and an employer.[1] There are eight terms—including salary, vacation time, and job assignment—to nail down, and each person has point values associated with each of the terms. Their individual goal is to each maximize their own points. Usually, the pairs of negotiators go down the list in order, trying to agree on each item. They quickly realize, however, that this strategy isn't going to work. At the end of the thirty-minute negotiation, some of the negotiators have come to a resolution and others have decided to walk away without a deal. Those who have reached an agreement fall into one of two categories: those who are eager to work together, and those who feel uncomfortable with the outcome. Some pairs end up with similar point totals at the end, while others have wildly different totals. So what happened?

The most common mistake in this negotiation is making inaccurate assumptions, and the most common assumption is that the recruiter and the candidate have opposing goals. The candidate assumes the recruiter wants the exact opposite of everything the candidate wants, when in actuality they have two objectives in common, two that are opposing, two that are much more important to the candidate, and two that are much more important to the recruiter. Though contrived, this case mirrors most situations in life. Parties often share interests, even when they believe they're on opposite sides of an issue, and some issues are usually more important to one person than to the other.

The key to a successful negotiation is to ferret out everyone's interests so you can maximize the outcome for everyone. This is easier said than done, since most people hold their interests close to the vest, believing this gives them a stronger negotiating position. But oftentimes this strategy is misguided, because in actuality what you want might be right in line with what the other party wants.

Let's take my recent experience purchasing a car. I assumed the salesperson wanted me to spend as much as possible, because I wanted to spend as little as possible. But I decided to test this assumption. While test-driving the car, I asked a lot of questions about the automobile industry, including how salespeople are compensated. I learned that this salesperson's commission had nothing to do with the price I paid. His bonus was based upon getting an excellent evaluation from each customer regardless of the price of the car. I told him that wasn't a problem for me, and that I'd be delighted to give him a fabulous review in return for a great price. We found a win-win situation. I would never have known or imagined that our interests were aligned unless I took the time to explore them.

The good news is that you get opportunities to negotiate every day and so have many chances to practice this skill. Here's a story illustrating that negotiations can happen anywhere. A couple of years ago I was in Beijing for a conference and my colleague, Ed Rubesch, met up with some of his students from Thammasat University in Thailand who were planning a sunrise trip to the Great Wall. That sounded fantastic, and I became intent on finding a way to see the Great Wall at sunrise, too. I thought such a trip would be easy to arrange, but for some reason it turned out to be nearly impossible. I started with the concierge at the hotel, then a local professor, and then the taxi drivers near my hotel. No one was able to help me with my quest. At the same time, I was talking up this idea with other colleagues, many of whom wanted to join the excursion. We agreed to meet in the lobby of the hotel at 3:00 a.m. for the trip, and it was up to me to make it happen. I wasn't going to let them down, but I had no idea what to do. I had used up all the obvious solutions.

Across the street from my hotel was a school that taught English, and I thought that at the very least I'd be able to find someone with whom I could speak. The receptionist suggested I talk with a seventeen-year-old student who was in the lobby. I introduced myself and sat down to chat with him. My goal was to negotiate with him so he would help me reach my goals. After a short time, I learned he was an accomplished student, musician, and athlete who was in the midst of applying to colleges. Eureka! I'd found the way I could help him. I told him that if he would help me get to the Great Wall at sunrise, then I would write a letter of recommendation for him for college. It sounded like a great deal to him, too. With a few hours of effort he solved my problem, and I was only too pleased to write a letter that described his initiative, creativity, and generosity. Together we created a wonderful win-win situation.

Stan Christensen, who teaches a course on negotiation at Stanford, has built his career around extracting the most value from negotiations.[2] He has found that most people leave a lot of value on the table because they make assumptions that aren't correct. Stan recommends looking for surprises when you negotiate, because surprises indicate you've made inaccurate assumptions. He also advises you to pick your negotiating approach based on the interests and style of the person with whom you're negotiating, not on your own interests. Don't walk into any negotiation with a clearly defined plan, but instead listen to what's said by the other party and figure out what drives them. Doing so will help you craft a positive outcome for both sides.

Being a parent offers endless opportunities to hone negotiating skills. For example, several years ago, Josh wanted to purchase a new bicycle. He was interested in competing as a road cyclist and "needed" a fancy new bike. He came to Mike and me and said, "I've done all my research and have found the perfect bike. It's really important to me." Our response was, "That's nice. . . There's no way we're going to spend that much money on a bike. We would be willing to spend half that amount. But perhaps you can find a way to make purchasing the bike more attractive to us?" I urged Josh to think of things he could do for Mike and me that would be worth the price of the bike. What could he do to make our lives easier?

He thought for a few days and came back with a proposal. He offered to do all of his own laundry and to both shop for food and cook dinner for the family three nights a week. Mike and I took this under consideration and decided it was a good deal. By doing his laundry and making dinner, he was saving us a lot of time, and he would be learning some important skills. We agreed to the deal. Josh got the bike and took his new responsibilities seriously. Like all parents, we've had many other opportunities to negotiate future "deals," which goes to show that the most important outcome of any negotiation is to get to the next negotiation. The first deal is just the beginning. If the first negotiation is fair and balanced, and both parties follow through on their commitments, then chances are the next negotiation will go even more smoothly. As mentioned several times, we live in a very small world, where repeat appearances are the norm.

There are some cases that offer no win-win solution, and it's actually better to walk away. Stan gives his students a case involving a real estate deal that demonstrates this point. When you uncover the interests of the different players, it's pretty clear there's no intersection between their goals, and walking away is the best choice. Despite this, most students strike a deal anyway, even though it's suboptimal for both parties. Many of us hold to the mistaken assumption that any deal is better than walking away. This certainly isn't always the case, and walking away from a deal should always be considered a viable option.

The best way to know whether you should walk away from a deal is to understand your other choices, so you can accurately compare them to the deal at hand. In negotiation lingo this is called a BATNA (Best Alternative to a Negotiated Agreement).[3] Always know your BATNA when you start to negotiate. Stan uses a case study involving Disney and a group of environmentalists to illustrate this point. Disney wants to build a new theme park and the environmentalists are opposed. They go around and around on what Disney could do to protect the environment while still building the park. The two sides are unable to reach an agreement, and the deal falls apart. The result? The new park isn't built. However, shortly thereafter, the land is sold to a developer who builds tract housing on the same spot. The impact of the housing is much worse than that of the theme park would have been. Had the environmentalists taken their BATNA into account, they would have realized that reaching a deal with Disney was the preferred outcome.

In general, to negotiate effectively you should work to understand your own goals as well as the goals of the other party, attempt to come up with a win-win outcome, and know when to walk away. It sounds simple, but it takes a lot of effort to master these skills and to ensure that both parties are satisfied.

Another valuable skill is the art of helping others. When I was in college I spoke with my parents about once a week. At the end of every call my mother would say, "What can I do to be helpful to you?" The generosity of this gesture made a huge impression on me. In most cases there was nothing she could do to be helpful, but just knowing she was willing to help if needed was comforting. As I got older, I have realized that we can all do this for our friends, family, and colleagues. When you ask others if you can help, they are always pleased that you offered. A small number will actually take you up on your offer, and the things they ask for are usually modest. On rare occasions, someone will ask for something that you can't or don't want to do. Even when you turn them down, they are grateful that you offered and graciously accept the fact that you aren't able to help.

I suggest that you try this approach sometime, if you don't do it routinely already. But you must be sincerely willing to help if your offer is accepted. As Guy Kawasaki says, "You should always try to be a 'mensch.'" He continues, "A mensch helps people who can't necessarily help them back. Of course, it's easy to be generous to someone whom you think will be able to help you, but being a mensch means helping others even if you're pretty sure they can't help you. You can call it karma if you like, but people who are generous and helpful to others are those that others want to help in return."[4]

I clearly remember when I didn't know how to do this. When I was a freshman in college there was a fellow in my class who had a physical handicap that required him to use crutches to walk. One day he slipped walking down a ramp to class and fell to the ground. As he was struggling to get up, I didn't know what to do. I felt uncomfortable walking by without helping, but I was afraid that if I approached him I would embarrass him by drawing attention to his disability. I felt the same way when a classmate lost his mother to a long illness. I didn't know what to say, fearing I would say something wrong, and opted to say nothing. Years later, I was running on campus at Stanford. It had rained the day before and I fell hard in some mud. Bruised, hurt, and muddy, I sat on the curb with tears streaming down my face. At least a dozen people walked by, and not one asked me if I needed anything. At that exact moment I knew what I should have said to the fellow who fell in front of class years earlier and to my classmate who lost his mother. All I needed was someone to ask, "Are you all right? Is there anything I can do for you?" It now seems so simple. It's remarkable that it took me so many years to figure out.

This lesson is just as relevant when dealing with strangers as when working on teams. Unfortunately, most of us spend so much time in situations where we're encouraged to win at someone else's expense that it's hard to get practice helping others. I remember the first week of college, when I asked a girl in my dorm to help me with a calculus assignment. Without skipping a beat, she said, "If I help you then you will do better than I will and you'll get in to medical school and I won't." I'm not exaggerating. She wasn't willing to help me because we might be competing four years in the future. Years later, I listen to my son lament that all of his classes are graded on a curve. This means that in addition to focusing on learning the material for an exam, he and his classmates have to think about how well they will perform relative to one another. This is a huge disincentive to helping each other.

After years of working in such an environment, I had no idea how to be a good team player. It took me a long time to realize that this competitive mind-set, where you win at someone else's expense, is completely counterproductive. Almost everything in life is done in teams, and those who don't know how to make others successful are at a huge disadvantage. The best team players go to great lengths to make others successful. In fact, the higher you reach within an organization, the less important your individual contributions become. Instead, your job becomes leading, inspiring, and motivating others. Most of your work is done by colleagues tasked with implementing your ideas. Therefore, if you can't work well with others, then your ability to execute diminishes. Successful team players understand what drives each person on the team and look for ways to make them successful. Additionally, great leaders figure out a way for everyone to play to his or her individual strengths.

I've been on teams in which everyone on the team feels as though he or she got the "easy" job. If you think about it, this is the perfect work environment. Each person is doing what he or she does best, and is extremely appreciative of what the other people on the team bring to the table. Everyone has a job perfectly tuned to his or her skills and interests. Everyone feels great about his or her contributions, and celebrates the contributions of others. The saying "paint the target around the arrow" summarizes this wonderfully. I first heard this from my colleague Forrest Glick. It had been a mantra in his group when he worked at Harvard University. The idea is that you should pick the most talented person you can—*the arrow*—and then craft the job—*the target*—around what he or she does best. If you allow really talented people to do what they do best, then the results are astonishing. They're fulfilled and, therefore, much more productive than if they were doing something that didn't fit their talents or interests. The key is putting together a team with the right complement of skills.

As a job candidate, your goal is to find out if the job you are exploring is right for you. That is, are you the right arrow for the target? Too often, we focus on just getting the job instead of figuring out if the job is a good match for our skills and interests and, more important, whether we can work with the other people on the team. One way to figure this out is to find a way to talk about topics besides the job at hand. A great way to do this is to include your hobbies and interests at the bottom of your résumé, a hook for the person interviewing you and an easy way to uncover shared interests. I've seen this happen time and again. It might be a common interest in Indian cuisine, a curiosity about your collection of petrified wood, the fact that you belong to the same fraternity, or that you competed in the same sport in school. These kinds of hooks will draw your interviewer in, and present you as a person rather than as a collection of work experiences. It's also a terrific way to find out more about your interviewer.

There is a big pothole that smart people often fall into—they rationalize doing the "smart" thing as opposed to the "right" thing. Randy Komisar, the author of *The Monk and the Riddle*, emphasizes that these two concepts are often confused. Intelligent people often overanalyze a problem, coming up with a solution that they think is in their best interest (the smart choice) but that isn't the right thing to do. He told a personal story to illustrate the point. Randy had a contractor who had worked on his house. The contractor did a terrible job, and the project required a lot of follow-up work to correct the mistakes. Long after the project was completed, the contractor called Randy and told him that he hadn't paid the final bill. Knowing how disorganized the contractor was, Randy was fairly confident he would never be able to prove this one way or another. But looking back over his own records, Randy found that indeed he had not paid the bill. It would have been easy to question the contractor's bookkeeping and to justify not paying the bill. However, Randy knew that, despite his frustration with the contractor's work, he owed the contractor the money. He wrote a check, knowing he did the right thing.

When I think about doing the right thing instead of the smart thing, I'm reminded of a legal case in which I served as a juror. It was a wrongful termination case, in which a woman accused her employer of firing her without cause just days before her stock options were going to vest. This case went on for ten very long weeks, and I had a lot of time to think about the "right" outcome. The law was on the employer's side, because the plaintiff was an "at will" employee who could be fired anytime, but it wasn't clear whether the employer had done the "right" thing with regard to the timing of her dismissal. The jury deliberated for days. In retrospect, the deliberation was so difficult because we were torn between the right and the smart decision. Ultimately, we ruled in favor of the plaintiff, but we gave her a much smaller award than she was requesting. I later learned that the judgment was appealed, and another trial ensued.

Both the contractor story and the trial story highlight the fact that there is a significant difference between doing the right thing and rationalizing a decision that's best for you. Your actions always affect how others see you, and, as mentioned innumerable times now, you will likely bump into these same people again. If nothing else, you can be sure they will remember how you handled yourself.

One of the biggest things that people do to get in their own way is to take on way too many responsibilities. This eventually leads to frustration all the way around. Life is a huge buffet of enticing platters of possibilities, but putting too much on your plate just leads to indigestion. Just like a real buffet, in life you *can* do it all, just not at the same time. One approach is to pick three priorities at any one time, knowing that these will change as your life changes. This concept is not new. In fact, the U.S. Marine Corps and other military services use the "Rule of Three" as a general principle. Through years of trial and error, they've found that most people can only track three things at once. As a result, the entire military system is designed to reflect this. A squad leader is in charge of three fire team leaders, a platoon leader is in charge of three squad leaders, and each company consists of three platoons. The military experimented with a Rule of Four and effectiveness dropped precipitously.

Limiting ourselves to three core priorities can feel frustrating. However, you can avoid the "Tyranny of the *Or*" (having to choose between this *or* that). Indeed some things must be done serially. For example, when you're a new parent you have to let other things slide. And when you face a massive deadline everything else falls to the side. However, there are many ways to satisfy more than one desire at once. For instance, if you love to cook and want to spend time with friends, you can start a cooking club. I met a woman several years ago who had a group called "Chop and Chat." Every Sunday six women got together to cook at a member's home. Each member brought the ingredients to make a different recipe that was then split into six large portions. Members took home six different main courses for the week. Chop and Chat was an inventive way for the women to cook together, socialize, and prepare meals for their families.

You too can find innovative ways to combine your work and other activities about which you feel passionate. Take venture capitalist Fern Mandelbaum, for example. You would assume that meetings with Fern would take place in her office. But Fern is also an avid athlete, so when you want to discuss a new venture with her, be prepared to join her for a strenuous hike.

Everyone who knows Fern knows to wear walking shoes and carry a bottle of water to a meeting with her. She finds that this strategy is a great way to really get to know each entrepreneur while also getting fresh air and exercise. Also, consider Linda Gass, an award-winning artist who specializes in painting on silk. In addition to her career as a painter, she is an avid environmentalist. Over the years she has found ways to combine her interests by using her artwork to communicate about important environmental issues.[5]

To summarize, with a little practice it's easy to avoid obstacles and potholes that people often place in their own path. One of the best ways is to always show appreciation to those who help you. Keep a stack of thank-you notes on your desk and use them frequently. Also, never forget that the world is very small and you will likely bump into the same people time and time again. Protect and enhance your reputation—it's your most valuable asset and should be guarded well. Learn how to apologize with a simple "I'm sorry." Keep in mind that everything is negotiable and learn to navigate toward an outcome in which all parties win. Try to play to other's strengths, making sure they're doing what they do best. And do the right thing, as opposed to the smart thing, so you'll be proud to tell your story later. Finally, don't take on too much, lest you disappoint yourself and those who count on you.

Chapter 9

WILL THIS BE ON THE EXAM?

I never use PowerPoint slides in my class, except on the first day when I describe what we'll cover over the ten-week quarter. The final slide lists my commitments and what I expect of the students. The last bullet point is, "Never miss an opportunity to be fabulous." I promise to deliver my very best in each class, and I expect the same from them. I also tell the students that I have no problem giving everyone an "A," but that the bar is set very high. This is the first and last time I mention this.

So what happens? The students consistently deliver more than I or they ever imagined. They embrace the idea of being fabulous with remarkable enthusiasm, and they raise the bar repeatedly as the quarter progresses. In fact, a couple of years ago I arrived at class a few minutes early and found one of my students sitting outside listening to her new iPod nano. I hadn't seen one before and asked to take a look. She handed it to me and turned it over. The back was engraved with the words, "Never miss an opportunity to be fabulous!" Apparently, when she ordered it online, she had the option of having it engraved. Instead of adding her name or contact information, she chose this message, which she wanted to remember every day. She certainly didn't do this for me; she did it for herself.

I've been remarkably surprised by the stickiness of this message. It's as though students are just waiting to get this instruction. They're hungry for permission to do their very best, to hit the ball out of the park and to shine their brightest. Unfortunately, in most situations this doesn't happen. We're encouraged to "satisfice." That is, we're subtly or not so subtly encouraged to do the least amount we can to satisfy the requirements. For example, teachers give assignments and clearly state what's required to get specific grades. The classic question posed to a teacher is, "Will this be on the exam?" Teachers hate this question. However, students have learned through years of reinforcement that all they need to do is meet the minimum requirement to get the grade they want. This happens at work as well, when bosses outline specific objectives for their staff and create rubrics and metrics for giving bonuses and promotions.

It's easy to meet expectations, knowing exactly what you will get in return. But amazing things happen when you remove the cap. In fact, I believe there's a huge pent-up drive in each of us to blow off the cap. Like a soda bottle that's been shaken, individuals who remove perceived limits achieve remarkable results.

Consider Ashwini Doshi, who I first met several years ago when, as a graduate student, she applied for a research assistant job in our department. Despite my openness, I was really taken aback when she walked into my office for the job interview. Ashwini is a beautiful woman, but she is only three and a half feet tall. Her voice is that of a little girl, but her ideas are those of a mature adult. I'm embarrassed to say that I didn't hire her for the position. This happens to Ashwini a lot. People are so surprised by her appearance that it usually takes several interactions before they're comfortable enough to see past her physical differences. I'm fortunate that she decided to take my course, because it gave me an opportunity to get to know her quite well. When another position became available in our group, I jumped at the chance to hire her. Ashwini's work was exemplary, she was a terrific team player, and she always went way beyond what was expected.

Born in Mumbai (formerly Bombay), Ashwini grew up in a household of nineteen—her father, his three brothers, their wives, all of their children, and her grandparents. She was born normal size, but by the time she was a year old, it was clear that she wasn't growing properly. The doctors in India weren't able to provide guidance on her care, so her parents sent X-rays of her tiny skeleton to specialists in the United States. The only medical option was to put bone extensions in each of her extremities, a process that would have required extensive surgery over six years. She also would have been bedridden for months at a time, which was out of the question for this very active young girl.

Ashwini was fortunate that her family was so open-minded and loving. In many families, someone so different would have caused great embarrassment and, so, been hidden away. But they didn't do this to Ashwini. In fact, she went to the best schools in Bombay and always excelled. She has a remarkably positive attitude, and from a young age felt strangely empowered by her differences. Ashwini still thinks of herself as a normal person living an extraordinary life.

Ashwini sincerely feels there's nothing she can't do and has demonstrated this time and again. She came to California all by herself to attend graduate school. In addition to the cultural differences and her physical limitations, she didn't know anyone when she arrived. Many of her friends encouraged her to stay put, saying life would be much easier for her in India. But she persisted. Once she arrived at Stanford, the only accommodation she received was a small step stool in her apartment that would enable her to reach the stove. Out of necessity, she figures out ingenious solutions to all the physical obstacles that face her every single day.

When I asked Ashwini about the problems she faces, she had a hard time coming up with any. She just doesn't see them. When pressed, she sited the difficulty of finding a driving school willing to accept her as a student. After years of depending on rides from friends and on public transportation, she decided to learn to drive and purchased a set of pedal extenders so she could reach the gas and brake pedals. It took dozens of calls before she found a driving school that would take her.

What is most impressive is that Ashwini always delivers more than 100 percent of what she's called upon to do. Her only regret? She actually wishes she had taken even more risks when she was younger. Despite all she has overcome, Ashwini still thinks she took the safe path. She embraces the idea that life isn't a dress rehearsal, and that you only get one chance to do the best job. Ashwini is the ideal model of someone who never misses an opportunity to be fabulous.

Being fabulous implies making the decision to go beyond what's expected at all times. On the flip side, if you do the least you can to meet a baseline expectation, then you're cheating yourself of that opportunity. This sounds like the lecturing of a school principal, but it's true. The collection of missed opportunities adds up, leading to a huge deficit. Imagine the difference between investing $100 with a 5 percent return versus investing the same $100 with a 105 percent return. The divergence in value continues to compound over time. This is what happens in life. You get out of life what you put in, and the results are compounded daily.

Bernie Roth, a Stanford mechanical engineering professor, does a provocative exercise at the d.school to highlight this point. He selects a student to come up to the front of the room and says, "*Try* to take this empty water bottle out of my hand." Bernie holds the bottle tightly and the student tries, and inevitably fails, to take it. Bernie then changes the phrasing slightly, saying, "*Take* the water bottle from my hand." The student then makes a bigger effort, usually without result. Prodding the student further, Bernie insists that the student *take* the bottle from him. Usually the student succeeds on the third attempt. The lesson? There's a big difference between trying to do something and actually doing it. We often say we're trying to do something—losing weight, getting more exercise, finding a job. But the truth is, we're either doing it or not doing it. Trying to do it is a cop-out. You have to focus your intention to make something happen by giving at least 100 percent commitment. Anything less and you're the only one to blame for failing to reach your goals.

Bernie also tells students that excuses are irrelevant or, to use the technical term—bullshit. We use excuses to cover up the fact that we didn't put in the required effort to deliver. This lesson is relevant in all parts of your life. There's no excuse for being late, for not handing in an assignment, for failing an exam, for not spending time with your family, for not calling your girlfriend, and so forth. You can manufacture an excuse that's socially acceptable, such as having too much work or being sick, but if you really wanted to deliver you'd figure out a way to make it happen.

These are harsh words, since we're all so used to generating and hearing excuses. Bernie acknowledges that making excuses, or giving reasons for not delivering, is socially acceptable because it makes you sound "reasonable." But even if you feel obliged to make excuses to others, you shouldn't make them to yourself. You need to come to terms with the fact that if you really want to accomplish something, it's up to you to do so. Make it a high priority or drop it from your list. To drive home this point, Bernie asks his students to write down their biggest goal and then to list every impediment that prevents them from reaching it. It typically takes several minutes to compose the list. He then challenges the students to see that the only item that should be on the list is their own name. We make excuses for not reaching our goals by blaming others and external factors for getting in the way or for not enabling us. Again, achieving is your responsibility from start to finish.

These exercises, and the lessons they deliver, reinforce the notion that you are ultimately in charge of your own life. You have no excuse for delivering anything short of your best effort at all times. A wonderful example is Chong-Moon Lee, a successful Korean American entrepreneur.[1] His story is a terrific example of pushing through every barrier in his path in order to reach his goals. Mr. Lee had been trained in law, business, and library science and assumed he would pass his life as a university librarian. However, he was pulled into his family's pharmaceutical business in Korea. Ultimately, the tension between the family members became so intense that Mr. Lee decided to leave the company. He came to Silicon Valley to begin a new career, selling American goods to Japan. He was making a decent living, and decided to buy each of his children a computer. He gave his son an IBM PC and his daughter an Apple IIe. In his traditional view, he assumed that his son needed a more "professional" computer since he was being groomed for a business career and that his daughter would use her computer for school. It turned out that both kids spent all of their time on the Apple computer. Mr. Lee saw the power of the Apple software and graphical interface, and was inspired to create a way for PCs to run Apple software. He thought the software could easily be developed in twelve months—it ended up taking six years. Mr. Lee put everything he had into this venture, Diamond Multimedia, which made graphics cards for PCs. At times he was so broke he ate the cabbage that grocery stores had thrown out. But he stuck with his goal and after fourteen long years Diamond Multimedia became the top producer of graphics accelerators in the United States. He believes his success comes from being able to focus with unrelenting persistence, and acknowledges that he put his heart and soul into everything he did.

Another example is Perry Klebahn, the snowshoe designer described previously. Perry is a master at delivering far beyond what's expected of him. He recently became the president of Timbuk2, a maker of messenger bags and luggage. The San Francisco–based company was faltering badly before Perry arrived, mainly because it had outgrown its capacity to deliver. The infrastructure was stretched to its limits, employees were working in islands of isolation spread among many buildings, and morale was low. Perry was brought in to turn around the business. He scrutinized the situation with an eye toward making every aspect of it top-notch. His first step was to consolidate employees under one roof, in an effort to build a stronger sense of community. He then took the management team on a seven-day wilderness expedition, during which they had to rely on each other in the rawest sense. This made office issues seem mundane by comparison. Next, Perry decided to reward employees in a way that reflected and reinforced the company's goals. Each month all employees fill out a survey about their interests and activities, and a name is drawn via a lottery. The chosen employee receives a custom messenger bag designed around his or her passions. The bags are wildly unique and a terrific physical artifact that demonstrates the creativity and innovation that are the hallmarks of the business.

Then, inspired by open-source design at companies like Mozilla, where the users are empowered and encouraged to improve the product, Perry opened up Timbuk2's design process to an online community, inviting customers to weigh in on the features for the next wave of products. Hundreds of customers participated in the process the first time around, looking at drawings and providing great ideas that stretched the boundaries of Timbuk2's products. The result is a constantly refreshed set of insights and ideas.

Timbuk2 would likely have become a successful company even if Perry's team had just taken steps to fix the broken infrastructure, but he pushed those limits in his quest to make the company fabulous.

Those who accomplish amazing feats, such as Chong-Moon Lee and Perry Klebahn, are often assumed to be competitive. Many guess they accomplished their goals at the expense of others. But, this certainly isn't the case. There's a significant difference between being competitive and being driven toward an objective. Being competitive implies a zero-sum game in which you succeed at someone else's expense. Being driven involves tapping into your own passion to make things happen. But many great leaders are inspired and motivated by the successes of those around them.

I would argue that to be successful in an entrepreneurial environment, it's more productive to be driven than to be competitive, and I designed a simulation exercise to highlight this point. In the exercise I divide a group into six teams. I then unveil five completed jigsaw puzzles, each with a hundred pieces.[2] Participants are allowed to see the puzzles for a minute or so, and then all the pieces from the five puzzles are dumped into a pillowcase and mixed up. All but a few pieces, which I hold back, are then randomly distributed to the six teams. Each team is also given twenty poker chips to use as currency. The teams are responsible for completing a puzzle within an hour. When the time is up, points are calculated. Each team counts the number of pieces in the largest completed section of the puzzle and receives one point for each piece. They then count the number of pieces in small islands of connected pieces and receive half a point for each piece. Each team that completes an entire jigsaw puzzle in an hour earns a twenty-five-point bonus.

Since there are fewer puzzles than there are teams, participants have to decide if they're going to compete, collaborate, or both to collect the necessary puzzle pieces. This situation is meant to mimic the real world: participants know all the pieces exist to complete the task, but no one team controls them all. Teams have to find ways to get the resources they need to be successful. Additionally, since there aren't enough puzzles for every team, some teams have to find an alternative way to create value. As in the real world, there are many different roles to be played within an ecosystem. Also, the world is not static. After the game begins, every ten minutes or so something happens. I might auction off the puzzle pieces that I held back, or sell photos of the completed puzzles, or require one person from each team to move to another team, taking a few puzzle pieces with him. The changing environment requires both creativity and flexibility.

In order to be successful, the teams must work together. They start the game by trading and bartering, trying to figure out how to maximize their own benefits without giving away too much. This requires balancing strategy with action, figuring out how to divide the labor among team members, and how to walk the line between competition and collaboration, all in an ever-changing environment. Since they know there are fewer puzzles than there are teams, at least one team has to decide to *not* build a puzzle and to instead take on a different role. Sometimes one team chooses to divide up and join other teams. Sometimes two or three teams merge. At other times a team may take on the role of broker, buying and selling puzzle pieces from the other teams. And sometimes all of the teams merge into one huge team and work on all of the puzzles together. I like to do this exercise with larger groups that I can divide into two or more ecosystems, each with six teams and five puzzles. Doing so allows different strategies to evolve in parallel, which makes for interesting comparisons afterward.

The very worst outcome results when all of the teams decide to compete against one another. They hold back puzzle pieces and refuse to trade pieces needed by other teams. These groups become so focused on winning that they all lose. Sometimes the teams actually acknowledge that they would do better if they collaborated, but ultimately decide to compete anyway. Competition is so built into our culture that it becomes the natural response. Additionally, those teams that work hard to make other teams lose end up losing themselves. For example, the first time I ran this simulation, one team decided to hold on to a handful of pieces that other teams needed. Toward the end of the hour they planned to sell them to the other teams. This backfired. When the time was up, the teams had spent so much time competing with each other that they weren't even close to completing a puzzle. This meant the final pieces didn't offer any additional value.[3]

This exercise offers a strong reminder that in environments where there are limited resources, being driven to make yourself and others successful is often a much more productive strategy than being purely competitive. Those who do this are better able to leverage the skills and tools that others bring to the table, and to celebrate other people's successes along with their own. This happens in sports as well as in business settings, which are both often thought to be purely competitive environments. For example, in *It's Not about the Bike,* Lance Armstrong provides details about how competitors in the Tour de France work together over the course of the race in order to make everyone successful. And many competitive companies, including Yahoo! and Google, embrace "coopetition" by finding creative ways to work together, leveraging each business's strengths.

When it comes to being fabulous, many businesses select one area where they really shine. BMW focuses on top-notch engineering; Walmart promises the lowest prices; Disneyland strives to be the happiest place on earth; and Nordstrom works hard to deliver a world-class customer experience. If you ask people familiar with the store what they think about Nordstrom, most will offer at least one story about the incredible service they have received.

I had an opportunity to meet with two of the three Nordstrom brothers, Erik and Blake, who now run the company, and learned how they instill their employees with customer-centric values. Surprisingly, there are no specific rules or secret recipes for providing an outstanding customer experience at Nordstrom. Essentially, after only a short orientation, salespeople are charged with using their best judgment in solving the problems that come their way, and are empowered to act on their customers' behalf. Because each salesperson is different, they deal with their customers in unique ways, leading to a wide array of approaches to similar challenges. There's also a culture of telling stories at Nordstrom, and great customer service stories serve as lessons and inspiration. By empowering employees to be inventive in solving problems, the Nordstroms also give them the freedom to make mistakes. Blake and Erik both pointed out that if an error is made in an effort to serve the customer, it's quickly forgiven—and the same mistake is rarely repeated.

At Nordstrom, all incentives are aligned to create a terrific customer experience. Each manager works to make his or her own team successful, and all employees view their customers as the ultimate "boss." The senior managers of the company, including Blake, Erik, and their brother Pete, spend half their time visiting stores, where they walk the sales floor, interact with customers, and talk with the sales personnel. They're very familiar with this environment, each having started his career working in the Nordstrom stockroom, selling shoes, managing shoe departments, serving as buyers, managing individual stores, and then as regional managers. Now, as leaders of this multibillion-dollar business, they're still constantly looking for ways to improve. They watch and listen carefully, with great humility, and then, based on the information they have gathered, act with confidence and conviction. They're so intent on continuing to enhance customer satisfaction that they've made it remarkably easy for any customer to reach each of them. All three brothers answer their own phones, read their own e-mail, and respond to messages personally.

The idea that the customer comes first is so embedded into the culture of Nordstrom that the brothers describe the organization as an upside-down pyramid, with the customer at the top and the senior management at the bottom. When you advance in the company, you literally move *down* the corporate ladder. There's also no chief executive officer at the bottom. Blake is the president, Erik is the president of stores, and Pete is president of merchandising. They work as a very tight team, each brother playing to his own strengths. They share a vision for the business and work in a concerted and collaborative manner.

My favorite customer service story from Nordstrom is of a customer who asked the men's department for two blue button-down shirts with white collars. The salesperson helping him couldn't find these in stock or at any of the other Nordstrom stores. But, instead of telling the customer they couldn't meet his request, she took two white shirts and two blue shirts to the store tailor and asked to have the collars switched so there were two blue shirts with white collars and two white shirts with blue collars. She presented the blue shirts to the customer and told him that if he wanted the reverse, that was now available, too!

Both Blake and Erik point out that every experience with each customer is like a fresh chance at bat. Each interaction is another opportunity to deliver a great experience for the customer and to enhance the salesperson's reputation. Even if their actions don't lead to a specific sale, the investment eventually pays off.

As you can see, being fabulous comes in many flavors, but it all starts with removing the cap and being willing to reach for your true potential. This means going beyond minimum expectations and acknowledging that you are ultimately responsible for your actions and the resulting outcomes. Life isn't a dress rehearsal, and you won't get a second chance to do your best.

Chapter 10

EXPERIMENTAL ARTIFACTS

I have a confession to make—I easily could have titled all of the previous chapters "Give Yourself Permission." By that I mean, give yourself permission to challenge assumptions, to look at the world with fresh eyes, to experiment, to fail, to plot your own course, and to test the limits of your abilities. In fact, that's exactly what I wish I had known when I was twenty, and thirty, and forty—and what I need to constantly remind myself at fifty.

It's incredibly easy to get locked into traditional ways of thinking and to block out possible alternatives. For most of us, there are crowds of people standing on the sidelines, encouraging each of us to stay on the prescribed path, to color inside the lines, and to follow the same directions they followed. This is comforting to them and to you. It reinforces the choices they made and provides you with a recipe that's easy to follow. But it can also be severely limiting.

In Latin America there is actually a phrase that translates into "jacket puller" to describe people who try to pull others down—presumably by the tails of their jackets—to prevent them from rising higher than they have. People in other parts of the world call this the "tall poppy" syndrome, where those who stand up taller than those around them are cut down to size. Staying with the pack is the norm, and those who get ahead risk being dragged backward by their community. Worse still, there are also regions of the world in which those who do things differently are literally viewed as criminals. In Brazil, for instance, the traditional word for entrepreneur, *empresario,* translates loosely into "thief." Historically, there are not many local role models for successful entrepreneurs, and others assume you've done something illegal if you've successfully broken the mold. This was a significant problem for Endeavor, the organization whose goal is to enhance entrepreneurship in the developing world. When they launched in Latin America, Endeavor told people they wanted to stimulate entrepreneurship and they were met with great resistance. In response, they literally coined a brand-new word, *emprendedor,* to capture the true essence of innovation and entrepreneurial spirit. It took several years, but eventually emprendedor entered the lexicon. Endeavor now faces a similar challenge in Egypt, where they again intend to create and promote a new word for entrepreneur.

At the d.school much of our work focuses on giving students permission to challenge assumptions and to stretch their imaginations by breaking free from traditional ways of thinking. Every assignment requires them to leave their comfort zones and engage anew with the world around them. The faculty poses the challenges, but we don't have the answers. Additionally, the d.school classroom space invites experimentation. All of the furniture is on wheels and moves about easily to create different workspaces. Each time students arrive, the space is literally configured differently. Bins of paper, wood, plastic, paper clips, rubber bands, colored pens, pipe cleaners, and tape invite them to build prototypes to bring their ideas to life. The rooms are filled with movable white boards covered with colored stickies for brainstorming. The walls are peppered with photos and artifacts from past projects that serve as inspiration for creative thinking.

Our students are given real, open-ended challenges. For example, they might be asked to figure out how to improve bike safety on campus, or to find a way to entice kids to eat healthier food. Besides these local projects, d.school students in the Design for Extreme Affordability class, taught by Jim Patell and Dave Beach, work with partners in developing countries to identify problems and determine how to solve them in a cost-effective way. This project has led to a number of exciting products that are already on the way to market. For example, one team designed a brand-new baby incubator, Embrace, after visiting hospitals in Nepal and finding that traditional Western baby incubators, whose original price tag was $20,000, were not well suited for the local environment. Many were broken or in need of unavailable parts. The operating instructions and warning labels were in a language foreign to the nursing staff. Most important, the majority of births occur in villages far from city hospitals with incubators. Therefore, premature babies who need to be kept warm with an incubator rarely get access to the help they need.

The team identified the need for a low-cost, low-technology incubator. Over the course of a few months they designed a tiny sleeping bag with a pouch-insert containing a special wax. The melting temperature of the wax is 37 degrees centigrade, the temperature needed to keep a newborn baby warm.[1] For just $20, as opposed to $20,000, parents or local clinics can now take care of a premature baby on site or in transit. They remove the wax insert and place it in hot water to melt the wax. The insert is then put into the insulated sleeping bag, where it stays warm for hours. When it eventually cools down, the wax can easily be warmed up again. No technical training is needed, no electricity is required, and the design is inexpensive enough to be deployed in underserved communities without access to urban hospitals.

The students leave these courses changed forever. They have a new appreciation for the power of paying attention to the problems in the world around them, and learn that they're empowered to fix them. As David Kelley, the founding director of the d.school, would say, "They are leaving with creative confidence."[2] They know they have permission—both explicit and implicit—to experiment, to fail, and to try again. What we must all recognize is that every one of us has the same permission—we just need to recognize that it's ours to grant and not something extended from outside.

The message that we each determine how we view the world was driven home to me in an unexpected way. A few years ago I took a creative writing class in which the professor asked us to describe the same scene twice, the first time from the perspective of someone who has just fallen in love, the second from the point of view of someone who has just lost a child at war. You were not allowed to mention falling in love nor the war. This simple assignment revealed how completely different the world looks depending on your emotional state. When I imagined walking through a crowded city in a state of bliss, my mind was focused on the colors and sounds and my view was expansive. When strolling through a similar scene in a depressed state, everything looked gray and all the imperfections, such as cracks in the sidewalk, jumped into focus. I couldn't see beyond my own feet, and the city seemed daunting, as opposed to stimulating. I dug up what I wrote for that assignment nearly a dozen years ago:

> Linda leaned over to admire the bouquet of peach-colored roses she had just bought. Her mind wandered fancifully from the flowers to the wonderful smell of fresh bread coming from the bakery next door. Standing to the side of the entrance was an amateur juggler. With

> his wildly colored costume, he attracted an audience of children who giggled each time he made a mistake. She watched a few minutes, and found herself giggling too. He finished his performance with a foppish bow toward Linda. She took a deep bow in return, and handed him a rose.
>
> Joe walked with his head down, protecting himself from the icy fog, as wind-whipped newspapers sailed through the air, slapping against the buildings before taking off again. "Step on a crack, break your mother's back. Step on a line, break your mother's spine." These words kept running through Joe's mind as he passed each crack that disrupted the rhythmic pattern of the sidewalk. The childhood taunt became a low drone in the back of his brain as he focused on the uneven path that stretched in front of him.

This was a valuable assignment not just for practicing my writing skills but for life in general, a poignant reminder that we choose how we view the world around us. The environment is filled with flaws and flowers, and we each decide which to embrace.

I shared some of the stories from this book with my father, who then decided to take some time to reflect on his most important insights, looking back over the eighty-three years of his life. Despite his currently comfortable position, his path was far from preordained. He moved to the United States when he was eight years old. His family escaped from Germany in the 1930s, and they arrived with essentially nothing. My father spoke no English and his parents didn't have enough money to support their two children, so he lived with relatives, with whom he couldn't communicate, until his parents could afford to bring him home. From these humble beginnings, my father built an impressive life and career, and retired as executive vice president and chief operating officer at a large multinational corporation.

Reflecting on his life, my father determined that his most important insight is that you shouldn't take yourself too seriously nor judge others too harshly. He wishes he had been more tolerant of mistakes he made and those made by others, and that he could have seen that failure is a normal part of the learning process. He realizes now that most of our errors are not earth-shattering, and shared the story that brought this home for him. Working at RCA early in his career, he and his team had a project that was going very badly. My father and his colleagues stayed up for days on end trying to fix the problems. Working to find a solution became their entire focus for weeks. Shortly after the project was successfully completed, the entire program was cancelled. Even though the project was the center of their universe, to others it was expendable. He learned many times over that most things in life, especially our failures, aren't as important as we think they are at the time.

My father also reminded me that success is sweet but transient. When you're in a position of influence, authority, and power, the benefits are wonderful. But once the position is gone, the perks evaporate. Your "power" comes from the position you hold. When you're no longer in that position, all that goes with it quickly fades away. Therefore, you should not define yourself by your current position nor believe all your own press. Savor the spotlight when you have it, but be ready to yield center stage when it's time to go. When you leave a job, the organization will go on without you, as you are not indispensable. Of course, you will leave a legacy of all you have accomplished, but that too fades with time.

Today, my father is also acutely aware of the joy of being alive. Several years ago he had a heart attack, and his implanted defibrillator is a constant reminder of his mortality. We all know intellectually that each day is precious, but as we grow older or deal with a life-threatening illness, this sentiment grows increasingly more palpable. My father works hard to make each opportunity stand out, to appreciate every moment, and to avoid squandering even a single day.

In looking for inspiration for this book, I literally and figuratively opened every drawer and looked into every closet of my life. In the process, I stumbled upon a canvas duffel bag I've been dragging around for thirty years. The two-foot-long bag is filled with "treasures" that seemed important to me over the years. When I was twenty, this bag was one of my few possessions. I carried it with me from college to graduate school and everywhere I've lived since. Though I rarely open it, I always know where to find it. The bag and its contents are a tangible link to my past.

When I opened the bag, I found a small collection of unremarkable rocks and shells from far-off beaches, faded photo IDs dating back through my years of high school and college, a stack of old letters, and some of my early "inventions," including prototyped LED jewelry that I crafted out of modeling clay and watch batteries. I also found a small notebook of poetry, titled "Experimental Artifacts."

When I wrote the poems in this book they represented the flip side of the organized scientific experiments I was performing in my neuroscience lab while in graduate school. One of the poems, called "Entropy," jumped out at me. This poem is about the process of constantly reinventing oneself, of always changing the game plan, and of taking risks without knowing what will happen. I wrote that poem in September 1983. At that time, the future was murky, filled with vast uncertainty because I couldn't see very far into the future. Twenty-five years later I see it differently. Uncertainty is the essence of life, and it fuels opportunity. To be honest, there are still days when I'm not sure which road to take and am overwhelmed by the choices unfolding in front of me. But I now know that uncertainty is the fire that sparks innovation and the engine that drives us forward.

Hopefully, the stories in this book underscore the idea that boundless possibilities result from extracting yourself from your comfort zone, being willing to fail, having a healthy disregard for the impossible, and seizing every opportunity to be fabulous. Yes, these actions inject chaos into your life and keep you off-balance. But they also take you places you couldn't even have imagined and provide a lens through which to see problems as opportunities. Above all, they give you growing confidence that problems can be solved.

The poem I wrote twenty-five years ago is a poignant reminder of the anxiety I experienced in my twenties when I looked ahead, not knowing what lay around the next curve. I wish someone had told me to embrace that uncertainty. As the stories in this book demonstrate, the most interesting things happen when you get off the predictable path, when you challenge assumptions, and when you give yourself permission to see the world as opportunity rich and full of possibility.

ACKNOWLEDGMENTS

Four years ago, when he turned sixteen, it dawned on me that Josh would be heading to college in only two years. I wanted to share with him what I wished I had known when I left home and when I started my career. So, I created a growing list of things I now know are critically important in making one's place in the world. This document resided on the desktop of my computer and whenever I remembered another lesson, I added it to the list. A few months after I started this project, I was asked to give a talk to students in a business leadership program at Stanford and decided to use these insights for inspiration. I crafted a talk called "What I Wish I Knew When I Was Twenty," in which I wove together these concepts with short video clips of entrepreneurial thought leaders who amplified these ideas. The talk resonated with them, and soon thereafter I was asked to give this lecture in other venues around the world. Buoyed by the enthusiastic response, I crafted a book proposal. But, busy with a zillion other things, I never sent it out to potential publishers.

Two years later, I was sitting on an airplane on an early morning flight from San Francisco, on my way to Ecuador. After breakfast was served, I started a conversation with the man sitting next to me, Mark Tauber. He is the publisher of HarperOne in San Francisco, and by the end of the flight we had found several common interests related to education and publishing. We stayed in touch and worked on a few small projects together. A year later, after I sent him a link to the Innovation Tournament Web site, Mark brought several of his colleagues to Stanford to learn more about what's happening on campus. By the end of lunch, Gideon Weil, a senior editor at HarperOne, suggested that it might be interesting to publish a book that captures the lessons coming out of our classes. I told him I had already written a book proposal on that subject. The good news was that within a few weeks I had a book contract. The challenge was that I had only four months in which to write the book.

With six weeks of travel coming up and a full plate of other commitments, I needed to draw upon everything and almost everyone I know to get this project done. I am incredibly indebted to *all* those people who helped make this project come to life in such a short period of time. They generously shared their successes and their failures, their disappointments and the lessons they learned. They gave me encouragement and suggestions, and they provided me with a wealth of provocative stories.

First, I want to call out all those people who talked with me about their lives and careers, and shared important insights they gained along the way. This includes Lisa Benatar, Soujanya Bhumkar, Steve Blank, Teresa Briggs, Peggy Burke, Tom Byers, Dana Calderwood, Stan Christensen, Sandra Cook, Michael Dearing, Ashwini Doshi, Debra Dunn, Alistair Fee, Nathan Furr, Steve Garrity, Linda Gass, Jeff Hawkins, John Hennessy, Quincy Jones III, Jeanne Kahwajy, Guy Kawasaki, Perry Klebahn, Randy Komisar, Chong-Moon Lee, Fern Mandelbaum, Karen Matthys, Kevin McSpadden, Tricia Lee, Blake Nordstrom, Erik Nordstrom, Elisabeth Pate Cornell, Jim Plummer, Bruce Ransom, Bernie Roth, Michael Rothenberg, David Rothkopf, Linda Rottenberg, Josh Schwarzepel, Jerry Seelig, Jeff Seibert, Carla Shatz, John Stiggelbout, Carlos Vignolo, Quyen Vuong, and Paul Yock.

I also want to thank all those entrepreneurial thought leaders who come to Stanford to share their experiences. I mined the STVP Entrepreneurship Corner Web site for lessons from the following speakers: Carol Bartz, Mir Imran, Steve Jurvetson, David Kelley, Vinod Khosla, Marissa Mayer, David Neeleman, Larry Page, and Gil Penchina. I also acknowledge Steve Jobs for his remarkable commencement address at Stanford in 2005.

My wonderful colleagues at the Stanford Technology Ventures Program and the School of Engineering deserve considerable credit for their contributions to this project. They provided me with access to a long list of fascinating people and opportunities, and have enriched my life tremendously. First, let me thank Tom Byers for inviting me to join him ten years ago. Tom has been a terrific role model, a fabulous colleague, and a great friend. Second, I want to call out my fantastic colleagues, Forrest Glick, Theresa Lina Stevens, and Bob Sutton, who provided valuable guidance on this book, and to acknowledge Laura Breyfogle, Kathy Eisenhardt, Riitta Katila, Tom Kosnik, Elisabeth Pate Cornell, and Jim Plummer, who make Stanford's School of Engineering a remarkable place to work. Finally, special thanks go to STVP's sponsors, whose generosity allows us to educate the next generation of entrepreneurs.

Also, I need to pay tribute to my inspirational colleagues at the Hasso Plattner Institute of Design at Stanford, or d.school. Specifically, I want to call out Michael Barry, Charlotte Burgess Auburn, Liz Gerber, Uri Geva, Julian Gorodsky, Nicole Kahn, David Kelley, George Kembel, Jim Patell, Bernie Roth, and Terry Winograd.

I also want to acknowledge all the students with whom I have the pleasure of working, including the Mayfield Fellows, BioDesign Fellows, the d.school Bootcamp and Summer College students, and all those in my course on Creativity and Innovation. Their entrepreneurial spirit consistently exceeds all of my expectations.

There are also several people who read this manuscript in various stages of its evolution and gave me valuable feedback. This includes James Barlow, Sylvine Beller, Peggy Burke, Katherine Emery, Carol Eastman, Gregg Garmisa, Jonah

Greenberg, Boris Logvinskiy, Patricia Ryan Madson, Juliet Rothenberg, Jerry Seelig, Lorraine Seelig, Robert Seelig, and Anand Subramani. Their comments and suggestions had a big influence on the book.

Even with all this inspiration and support, this project would never have materialized without the guidance provided by Gideon Weil at HarperOne. He is a remarkable coach, a terrific teacher, and wonderful editor. I learn something new in every one of our conversations and always look forward to his calls. Additionally, I want to thank Lisa Zuniga for editing the book. She worked with me, at breakneck speed, to make sure that the nuances of all the stories were not lost as she polished the prose. And, special thanks goes to Mark Tauber for befriending me on that cross-country flight several years ago. That story is a powerful reminder that you never know what will happen when you strike up a conversation.

On a personal note, I want to give a huge shout-out to my parents, who laid the foundation of my education. They have been wonderful role models and teachers my entire life. Additionally, my husband, Michael Tennefoss, has been a terrific partner and a valuable advisor while I was writing this book. He listened carefully as I read each chapter no matter what time of day I finished writing, was the first editor of the manuscript, and always provided candid feedback along the way. I am forever indebted to Michael for his helpful suggestions, unconditional support, and unending encouragement.

Finally, I am thankful to Josh for inspiring me to make a list of things I wish I knew when I was his age. Over the past four years, Josh has chimed in with his thoughtful responses to the concepts in this book, and I continue to be awed by his wisdom. This book is my twentieth birthday present to Josh. Happy Birthday . . . and many more!

NOTES

CHAPTER 1 : BUY ONE, GET TWO FREE

1. You can find details about the one red paper clip project at http://www.oneredpaperclip.com.
2. You can watch winning videos from the Innovation Tournaments on the STVP Entrepreneurship Corner Web site, at http://ecorner.stanford.edu. Search for "tournament" to find them. This Web site contains a growing collection of thousands of video clips and podcasts on entrepreneurship, leadership, and innovation.
3. The *Imagine It* movie can be downloaded for free at http://www.imagineitproject.com.
4. You can watch video clips of Vinod Khosla at http://ecorner.stanford.edu.
5. The Stanford Technology Ventures Program is hosted by the Department of Management Science and Engineering within Stanford's School of Engineering. The program Web site is http://stvp.stanford.edu. This site includes links to all the STVP courses, research projects, and outreach efforts.
6. I first heard the concept of T-shaped people from my colleagues at IDEO, a premier design consulting firm in Palo Alto, California.

7. The d.school Web site is http://dschool.stanford.edu It includes extensive information about the Hasso Plattner Institute of Design.

CHAPTER 2: THE UPSIDE-DOWN CIRCUS

1. You can find out more about the BioDesign Program at http://innovation.stanford.edu.

2. You can watch video clips of Paul Yock at http://ecorner.stanford.edu.

3. This two-part case study is available through the European Case Clearing House. The titles are: "The Evolution of the Circus Industry" and "Even a Clown Can Do It: Cirque du Soleil Recreates Live Entertainment."

4. You can watch video clips of Randy Komisar at http://ecorner.stanford.edu.

5. You can watch video clips of Guy Kawasaki at http://ecorner.stanford.edu.

CHAPTER 3: BIKINI OR DIE

1. "Selection by Consequences," *Science*, vol. 213, 31 July 1981.

2. You can watch video clips of Larry Page at http://ecorner.stanford.edu.

3. You can find details about Endeavor at their Web site: http://www.endeavor.org.

4. This exercise is a modification of a project used by Terrence Brown, who used to teach at the Royal Institute of Technology (KTH) in Stockholm, Sweden.

5. You can watch video clips of Armen Berjikly at http://ecorner.stanford.edu.

6. You can watch video clips about Moto Restaurant on Youtube.

CHAPTER 4: PLEASE TAKE OUT YOUR WALLETS

1. You can watch video clips of Debra Dunn at http://ecorner.stanford.edu.
2. You can watch a seven-minute video summarizing this exercise at http://ecorner.stanford.edu. Do a search for "wallet" to find it.
3. You can watch video clips of David Rothkopf at http://ecorner.stanford.edu.

CHAPTER 5: THE SECRET SAUCE OF SILICON VALLEY

1. You can find the entire GEM report at: http://www.gemconsortium.org.
2. "Spain's Showy Debt Collectors Wear a Tux, Collect the Bucks," *Wall Street Journal*, October 11, 2008.
3. You can watch video clips of Steve Jurvetson at http://ecorner.stanford.edu.
4. The Mayfield Fellows Program Web site is http://mfp.stanford.edu.
5. You can watch video clips of Mir Imran at http://ecorners.stanford.edu.
6. You can watch video clips of Bob Sutton at http://ecorner.stanford.edu.
7. You can watch video clips of Gil Penchina at http://ecorner.stanford.edu.
8. You can watch video clips of Carol Bartz at http://ecorner.stanford.edu.
9. You can watch video clips of David Neeleman at http://ecorner.stanford.edu.
10. You can watch video clips of Marissa Mayer at http://ecorner.stanford.edu.

CHAPTER 6: NO WAY . . . ENGINEERING IS FOR GIRLS

1. There is an important caveat here: If you're dedicated enough, it's worth trying to build a market around your passions and your skills. Think of new artists or musicians who have generated public interest in their work. If you're creative and work hard, there is often a way to open up a whole new market. There is a story later in the book about Perry Klebahn, who does just this by creating demand for his new snowshoes.

CHAPTER 7: TURN LEMONADE INTO HELICOPTERS

1. You can listen to a podcast with QD3 and MC Hammer at http://ecorner.stanford.edu.
2. You can watch the video with the basketball players and the moonwalking bear here: http://www.youtube.com/watch?v=2pK0BQ9CUHk.

CHAPTER 8: PAINT THE TARGET AROUND THE ARROW

1. I modified this exercise from one done by Maggie Neal at the Stanford Graduate School of Business.
2. You can watch video clips of Stan Christensen at http://ecorner.stanford.edu.
3. The concept of having a BATNA—Best Alternative to a Negotiated Agreement—was first described by Roger Fisher and William Ury in the book *Getting to Yes*.
4. *Mensch* is Yiddish for someone who is admired and trusted and whose opinion is sought out by others.
5. You can see Linda Gass's paintings at http://www.lindagass.com. She has a new series of paintings devoted to water issues in California.

CHAPTER 9: WILL THIS BE ON THE EXAM?

1. You can watch video clips of Chong-Moon Lee at http://ecorner.stanford.edu.

2. I was inspired to design this game after hearing about another game using jigsaw puzzles from my colleague Carlos Vignolo from Chile. His game runs forty-eight hours.

3. You can watch a five-minute video that summarizes the two-hour exercise by going to http://ecorner.stanford.edu and doing a search for "puzzle."

CHAPTER 10: EXPERIMENTAL ARTIFACTS

1. When they were doing early experiments, the Embrace team used margarine instead of wax. It is inexpensive and easily obtained, and the temperature at which it melts is very close to body temperature.

2. You can watch video clips of David Kelley at http://ecorner.stanford.edu.